HOT H

The Body Electric

HOT HOT HOT!
The Body Electric

ANNE HOOPER

BOOKS

This edition first published in Great Britain in 2007 by JR Books, 10 Greenland Street, London NW1 0ND
www.jrbooks.com

Copyright © 2007 Anne Hooper

First edition published in Great Britain by Virago Limited, 1980; published in paperback by Unwin Paperbacks in 1984 and by Pandora Press in 1991.

Anne Hooper has asserted her moral right to be identified as the Author of this Work in accordance with the Copyright Designs and Patents Act 1998.

The fantasty on pages 146–7 reproduced with permission from *My Secret Garden* by Nancy Friday.

A catalogue record for this book is available from the British Library.

ISBN 978 1 906217 06 9

1 3 5 7 9 10 8 6 4 2

Printed in the UK by CPI Bookmarque, Croydon, CR0 4TD

Contents

This is the female form,
A divine nimbus exhales from it from head to foot,
It attracts with fierce undeniable attraction,
I am drawn by its breath as if I were no more than a helpless vapor, all falls
   aside but myself and it,
Books, art, religion, time, the visible and solid earth, and what was expected of
   heaven or fear'd of hell, are now consumed,
Mad filaments, ungovernable shoots play out of it, the response likewise
   ungovernable,
Hair, bosom, hips, bend of legs, negligent falling hands all diffused, mine too
   diffused,

Ebb stung by the flow and flow stung by the ebb, love-flesh swelling and
   deliciously aching,
Limitless limpid jets of love hot and enormous, quivering jelly of love, white-
   blow and delirious juice,
Bridegroom night of love working surely and softly into the prostrate dawn,
Undulating into the willing and yielding day,
Lost in the cleave of the clasping and sweet-flesh'd day.

This the nucleus – after the child is born of woman, man is born of woman,
This the bath of birth, this the merge of small and large and the outlet again.

Be not ashamed women, your privilege encloses the rest, and is the exit of
   the rest,
You are the gates of the body, and you are the gates of the soul.

The female contains all qualities and tempers them,
She is in her place and moves with perfect balance,
She is all things duly veil'd, she is both passive and active,
She is to conceive daughters as well as sons, and sons as well as daughters.

As I see my soul reflected in Nature,
As I see through a mist, One with inexpressible completeness, sanity, beauty,
See the bent head and arms folded over the breast, the Female I see.

I Sing the Body Electric
Walt Whitman

INTRODUCTION

Thirty years ago, determined to change the world, I wrote a book called *The Body Electric*. Women would no longer suffer from ignorance about sex. Females who didn't have a clue about orgasm would learn how to have them and what a fantastic experience they could be. I'd had a tough time myself for a brief period when hormone changes rendered me sensationless. So I did have some inside knowledge of what many women suffered from *all the time*. And I really wanted to do something about it.

I got together with a like-minded friend and together we started running pre-orgasmic groups. After the first two I realised that disseminating sex information this way was like throwing water into the sea. My methods needed to become more encompassing. So I wrote the first edition of this book on the grounds that a book lasted and could be read by anyone over the years.

And for a long while that is what happened. Thousands of women read the book. One enthusiast was kind enough to describe it as 'a seminal work'. Another turned it into a play. As a result of women's apparent greater comfort with the subject, newspapers and magazines subsequently seemed unable to leave the word 'orgasm' out of their copy. I really thought the word had spread.

I became an Agony Aunt and had columns in several best-selling magazines and ended up as the first regular writer on the subject of sex for the UK's highly conservative newspaper, the *Daily Mail*. Job done, you might think.

HISTORY REPEATS ITSELF

So imagine the disappointment when history repeated itself. My youngest son, Alex, also became an Agony Uncle (he writes for *Sugar* – a best-selling magazine for very young women). Every so often he passes one of his columns across to his aged parents for our comments. To my real dismay the young women writing in to him were asking identical questions to the ones I thought we had bopped on the head all those years ago.

What I've learned from this is that there seem to be cycles of knowledge. Just as one generation has absorbed a message the next generation comes along with the same anxiety, lack of confidence and lack of intimate knowledge. It's not that they can't talk about sex these days. They can. That much has seeped through into people's consciousness. But what is still difficult (maybe it always will be) is talking about the intimacy of sex – about what actually goes on between two people and, more importantly for the theme of this book, what goes on between you and your genitals in the privacy of your own bedroom.

When Eleanor and I started the groups, I was working in a clinic for sexual dysfunction, plus I had experienced one of sex educator extraordinaire Betty Dodson's groups in New York – an event never to be forgotten. Eleanor had recently returned from Los Angeles where she had worked with Lonnie Barbach, a denizen of sex therapy for women. Between us we decided on a combination of verbal information, group sharing and actually experiencing several physical events. England, by comparison with the US, has always been a bit backward when tackling physicality, so what we were doing felt daring for the time. On re-reading, some of the group content *still* feels daring by *any* time.

A NEW METHOD OF WRITING

The groups took place over a six- to eight-week period (depending on our experiments) – we met once a week for two-hour sessions and between sessions, the women had extensive homework that was vital to the course. So, when I came to write this book, I structured the writing like a group. I was influenced in the 1970s by the journalism of Tom Wolfe, who at the time had invented something that went by the name of 'New Journalism', which consisted of factual reports written as if they were fiction. Not many journalists had done this before and the style of writing had the effect of pitching you into the battle or the natural disaster that he was describing. As the reader you felt what he was relating. It meant something.

Why couldn't you write a handbook that worked in the same way? I decided to give it a try. Each chapter of the book consists of a week in the life of the group. During that week you hear the stories of each woman attending the group, you learn with them and, at the end of the week (chapter), you are given the homework for each woman to do during the interim. In this way you become the seventh participant in the group. You can both learn from their experiences and share in their homework by doing it yourself.

You can use the book as an individual in private, or you can use it as a guide to holding your own group.

A small but rapidly growing young publisher, Virago, published the first edition, which conferred status on my slim volume. And it succeeded. Thousands of copies were sold. It went on to be re-published on two further occasions. Extracts were taken from it and appeared in compilations of erotic poetry.

But for the past ten years it has been assumed that young women know it all when it comes to sex. How could they not be fully *au fait* when a blitz of sex info reins down upon them from magazines, TV and newspapers? Which brings us neatly to my son and his agony letters. On behalf of every young woman, therefore, who is longing to experience that elusive sensual experience which she reads so much about and yet, so far, escapes her, here is a re-written, updated version of what is slowly becoming a classic read.

THE WOMEN IN THE GROUP

Even if you don't have difficulties with sex, finding out what happened to the six women who took part in this particular group can be gripping. I should explain here that, with one exception, the six women are composites of several women although everything in the stories reported here really happened. The exception is Kate, whose story is complete, happened in full and is truly and faithfully described. Names have been changed and the language slightly altered to bring the story up to date.

The final day of each group is a sad occasion. Emotional ties between us have been so strong that several groups refuse to disband. Long after the original course has ended, they are still meeting. One group persisted in learning massage skills; another brought their partners along for mixed meetings. There's always a demand for an 'advanced' course.

Perhaps most important of all has been the rediscovery of the delight of masturbation. Masturbation, since Victorian days, has been put down successively as evil, harmful, draining vital juices or, at best, second best. In fact, it can be a triumphant explosion or slow, drawn-out ecstasy. It's a wonderful experience in its own right. It's free, fulfilling and simply requires the power of our fingertips (or occasionally the power of 40 watts). It beats the hell out of the TV, cocoa and early nights!

Chapter 1

WEEK ONE

Apprehensive glances around the flat, the smell of coffee drifting through the little room and six women wishing they'd gone to a Pilates class instead.

The grim, almost scowling nerves of the first half hour of the first meeting have a lot in common with the prowling tension of an abortion ward before the op. Yet when the same women say goodbye at the end of this, their first session, their relief, by contrast, is almost joyful. 'I'm really looking forward to coming next week.'

As soon as people arrive we occupy them, giving them as little time as possible in which to be fearful. They fill in a biographical sheet on which they tell us who they are living with (if anyone), how many brothers and sisters they have, the age at which they first remember masturbating, the number of sexual relationships they've had and, if they have a partner, what are his/her reactions to their joining the group. They quickly drink the coffee put in front of them.

Women are always late for this first meeting. They're scared. But at a quarter to eight we begin.

The eight of us (Jo assists me as well as owning the flat) are seated on cushions in a circle. So far there's been an embarrassed silence punctuated only by self-conscious remarks that quickly tail away. Now we break the ice in a rush. The women pair off and spend five minutes telling each other the 'facts' about themselves: why they are here, what they want from the workshops, what their background and family life are like, what they think about their parents and upbringing.

The room now hums with voices and the women relax, gesticulate and begin to feel expectant, which is half the purpose of the exercise. The other half is to prepare them for the next round, where facing the circle, they tell us all an expanded version of what they've recounted to their neighbour.

The Meaning of Family Dynamics

There are reasons, of course, for getting the women to think back to childhood. What we learn as children unconsciously shapes how we construct our later lives and most especially our sex lives. We tend to expect (even if we don't realise it) that our own relationships will follow a pattern similar to our parents'. So particular people in the family, special circumstances, traumatic events and differing morality during childhood are all dynamics of childhood that affect how we function today. As the women in the group reveal their stories they will hopefully make connections they've never made before and gain insight into their relationships, personalities and expectations.

THE WOMEN

JAN

Jan, aged 28, has come with a friend. She's a pretty woman, slightly overweight and possesses limbs that seem to be made of India rubber. She sits effortlessly cross-legged in the lotus position, a posture that her neighbour tries to copy but which immediately makes her fall down. Jan explains that she practises yoga and wants to teach it. She tells us that she can have orgasms through mastur-bating and has been happy to do this since the age of four. But she has *never* experienced an orgasm while making love with a partner.

Jan's mother was warm and demonstrative towards her when she was a child. But her father was remote (he had never touched her physically, either to hug or even pat her), though Jan knew that he cared for her.

'I've always had a nagging feeling that I disappoint him, however hard I try,' she tells us. 'I constantly need to prove to Dad that I'm a fully functioning human being, that all of me is there. But now I'm older I suppose I've given that up a bit. And from going through several experiences, which were bound to antagonise him, I've finally had to accept that I'm just very different from him. I'm trying to learn to feel all right with being me, instead of feeling constantly guilty that I'm not what *he* would like me to be.'

The experiences Jan was talking about are those of living with her partner without being married and having a child (Will, her son, is two), a common enough situation in the 21st century but thoroughly disapproved of by a very traditional, older dad.

'I used to feel a lot of relief at being able to have orgasms by masturbating,' she continues. 'But now I worry that I do it too much, that it's becoming obsessive. And I'm scared there's something wrong with me as a woman because I can't have climaxes with Jim.'

How does Jim feel about it? 'He's never been happy about it. He complained. I thought it would help if I could say, "Look, babe, it's OK. I think you're marvellous, don't worry about the climaxes. I can get them for myself. Let's do it that way for me." But he hated it. "You're telling me I'm doing something wrong," he'd say continually. "You're telling me it's my fault, when it's not, it's yours." And unfortunately I think he's right. I've had at least ten other boyfriends and I've never come with any of them either. I've never lived with any of them, though, so it hasn't mattered much before.

'We've been living together for three years now and the relationship has got pretty bad. There are loads of times when I think to myself, "You'd be better off without him". But I just can't split with him. First off, he's Will's father. Second, I find him so sexually attractive I can't imagine ever finding any other man so marvellous to look at. And I don't want to do without that. I'm hooked on him.

'I'm pretty unhappy, though. I don't feel important to *anyone* and my sexuality is withering away. I'm only 28 for God's sake! Jim tells me continually that no one else would be interested in me, that I'm a frigid bitch and that he's doing me a big favour by staying with me. The trouble is that although I hate him saying this, deep down, I think he's probably right. I'm pretty scared.'

Further probing reveals that Jan is financially independent, has always worked, even after her child was born, is sole owner of the flat they live in and is not supported by Jim, who is a mainly out-of-work rock musician. In fact, since he tends to be in and out of work, she funds him.

For such an (on paper) independent being, Jan is surprisingly hesitant. When she describes her problems she is halting and unsure, and her obvious need to please is at odds with her healthy, sexy, outgoing appearance. It's as if she has all the ingredients of a very confident woman but couldn't learn the recipe to mix them successfully.

The Impact of Derision on Self-Belief

You may be outwardly the most effective, glamorous high-achiever possible, yet inwardly suffer from a crushing lack of self-assurance. One noted cause of such a split is when childhood has been punctuated by vicious invective and derision. As a child, Jan felt she could never do well enough and her partner has picked up on this, using put-downs and criticism as a form of control. Jan needs to see this for herself, however. If you are constantly told that you are hopeless and that you will never do well, it becomes very hard to think otherwise. Message to all parents: build up your child's self-esteem!

MAXIE

Sitting next to Jan is her friend Maxie. Maxie is 38. She's tall, thin and elegant. Her black shiny hair is sleek and her fingernails an immaculate deep red. At initial glance I wonder if she is a model or a fashion editor. She certainly gives the impression of being a high-powered career woman, whose life is organised exactly as she wants it. But if there's one thing that running these groups has taught me, it is that appearances can be mightily deceptive.

In reality, Maxie is a competent typist, working at a fashionable private London hospital. But she hates the job. She's in a typing pool with much younger women and feels she's getting nowhere with her career. She feels much the same about her sex life. She has never experienced orgasm, has had a series of brief love affairs with men and has had only one permanent relationship during which she lived with a lover for two years.

It has never occurred to Maxie that masturbation might be a nice or a useful thing to do. She is an only child who had very few close friends either as a child or a teenager. Her father died years ago. Her mother is still alive but lives in the country and Maxie doesn't see her often. In the past six years Maxie has had two nervous breakdowns, going home to live with her mother for a short time after the second. Now she frequently gets depressed and still regularly visits a counsellor. She never contributes spontaneously to the group. On the other hand, when she is specifically asked to do so, she talks confidently and fluently.

'I do have a boyfriend, Don,' she tells us, 'But he's not really a special boyfriend. He's just someone I go out with. I don't think he's very interested in whether I climax or not. I'm here because I've realised it's ridiculous at 38 not to do something about my lack of orgasms. If I don't do something about it, I can't see that anyone else is going to.

'And although I know the obvious things about sex, I realise, through talking to Jan, that there's an awful lot I don't know. And I'd like to. It's fair to say that if Jan hadn't come, I wouldn't have either.'

Only Child/Isolated Childhood Syndrome

An interesting statistic to emerge after ten years of running pre-orgasmic groups was that the women who had never experienced orgasm had often lived unusually isolated childhoods. Maybe they were situated miles away from others, or were single children in a very sheltered family. But what came across was a lack of knowledge, an ignorance about sex that most other young women don't have. You would think that in a blitz of sex programmes on television and in magazines, no one could possibly be sexually ignorant today. This turns out not to be true. As soon as I hear someone has had a lonely or sheltered childhood, I explore the possibility that they need detailed sexual information.

MAGGIE

Maggie is a quiet, shy woman, aged 26 and single. 'I lived with someone for five years and then he went abroad two years ago. There hasn't been anyone else since then.' She is very pale-skinned, looks as if she has not stepped outdoors for years, and has straggly dark hair that isn't too clean.

Since her boyfriend's departure Maggie has filled her life with evening classes and drinking with old friends (all women) whom she went to school with. Her life sounded pretty busy and it didn't seem as if she missed having a partner.

Her voice is very tiny and childlike when she's not sure of the impact she might be making. But when contributing something she feels strongly about, it becomes deeper and much more forceful. She sounds, in fact, like another person.

'My parents have virtually no physical contact with each other at all,' she tells us. 'They never cuddle or show affection towards each other. I think that's because there *isn't* much affection between them. My father railroads my mother in anything she ventures an opinion on and has no respect for her of any sort. He did the same thing to me until I was about 20. Then I started standing up to him. We had dreadful fights. But however hard I argued, absolutely nothing I said could win any change in his attitudes. To my father, women are a second-class sex. I gave up fighting.

'But I could and did leave home. The trouble with that was that I hated leaving my mother to bear the brunt of his rudeness and dismissiveness. At least my presence had dampened down his cruelty and given her a sense of value as a mother. Now I'm frightened for her. I see her retreating further and further into her shell.

'It's hard for me to show affection. Joe, my boyfriend, used to complain about the difficulties I found in giving him a cuddle. It wasn't that I didn't like doing it. It just never spontaneously occurred to me that it would be a nice thing to do. Perhaps that's because I never saw anyone else do so, certainly not Mum and Dad.

'I do masturbate, have done so ever since I was a child. But I don't seem to come. I get to a pitch where I'm very excited, get lovely feelings and then it all goes away. I don't feel frustrated afterwards. But I do feel there ought to be more to sexual life than a few faint tremors. Perhaps they actually are orgasms but if they are, they're a let-down because they're nothing special.

'Perhaps I *am* really climaxing but I can't let myself go enough to be sure. I did once think I had an orgasm when I was in a swimming pool but my boyfriend said that would be impossible... I don't know what to think.'

Lack of Loving Example

How do you know how to be loving if you have *never* ever seen anyone demonstrating love? Suppose that you yourself have never been hugged or stroked or kissed as a child. How do you get to understand its impact and its meaning? Unloving parents have a lot to answer for with their lonely little sons and daughters.

MARY

Mary is a red-haired woman with a freckled complexion and fantastic skin. She's wearing a maternity smock because she's still breast-feeding her five-month-old baby. Aged 33, Mary has two children, the eldest being three years old. Mary's husband sounds very sexually demanding, not because he has a high sex drive (necessarily) but because he equates making love with *being* loved. And since he was starved of affection as a child, he demands it constantly from his wife. He wants sex all the time.

'Which means that every time I say I don't want to make love, he thinks it's a personal rejection. It's not. It's simply that I don't seem to want it as much as he does. How often does he want intercourse? At least every night – sometimes two or three times a day.' Mary is not orgasmic – at all.

'I've got to feeling very angry that he pursues me all the time. It's like he doesn't see the human being that is me, he just sees a fuck object – something that lets him feel better. And yet, I must emphasise, he does love me. I know that's true. It's as if the love and sex are running along two separate channels.

'I can't relax to enjoy myself with him over anything because the minute I begin to look happy he wants us to go to bed. I think I possibly could feel sexy if he'd let me have my own time. I'd love to want to make advances to him, but I'm never given the opportunity to want anything. He's always there, looking hopeful.

'I love him. He's a marvellous man. We can talk about anything. But talking doesn't give us any ideas on how to change this. Some friends have said that I should take a lover but that's the last thing I want. Anyway, I'm scared that I'd not be able to respond to someone new either.'

Mary has never tried to masturbate. 'Of course I know about it. But I couldn't do that to myself. Sex has always been to me something that two people should do together. Masturbating seems like a "lesbian" activity. And I'm not gay.'

Why does masturbation seem a lesbian activity? 'Well, it's what women do to each other when they can't get a man, right?'

Coping with two very young children is a tiring activity and, as Maggie describes her home life, a pattern of sexlessness emerges that coincides with pregnancy, young babies and desperate fatigue. Ironically, it sounds as if her husband's urgent need for affection is aggravated by the fact that, like Maggie, she finds it very hard to be outwardly demonstrative. 'My parents thought it was sissy to kiss and hold hands. I remember my mother saying so. I certainly don't think the same, because I love someone cuddling me. And I make sure I cuddle my babies. But I don't seem to tune into the occasions when I ought to be cuddling my old man.'

The Impact of Babies on Sex

It's ironic that at a time in your life when you may feel passionately loving, your body is too tired and too hormone-depleted to carry through your desires. It's also very tough on a husband who needs more physical loving than most, if sex is what reassures him. One natural reaction is that he pleads for intercourse and this, of course, becomes extremely pressurising, turning you off sex even more.

HALEY

Haley is a 25-year-old agency nurse, married to a social security officer. She's sexily dressed in a low-cut chemise and is very vivacious. She and Len have been married for three years, have no children and are very open with each other over marriage problems and sexual matters.

'We have sex often,' she tells us. 'We sometimes make love on the living room carpet at odd times of the day. He makes me feel very sexy. But I think I've only ever come with him twice. And each time the orgasm has been very faint. Len buys sex manuals and we read them together. I've taught myself to masturbate from them and I get very turned on by some of the stories. But although the masturbation feels nice, I don't climax with it.

'I don't think I have any problem with feeling sexy. I get turned on by porn sites on the Web but it's the experience of orgasm that's leaving me high and dry. Len has been very keen for me to come here. He's very supportive. He hasn't had other lovers, but he did once help me to go to bed with a woman I fancied very much. He took the husband off to a pub so that she and I could get together. It was very exciting. In fact, we met up on a couple of occasions. I still didn't come, though.

'Len and I are very loving and cuddly to each other. When we're making love, sometimes I know I am near to orgasm. But then part of me seems to turn off at that realisation. I do find it hard to relax because I feel Len is watching me. That tends to turn me off. I am frightened that Len is going to get so upset by my never climaxing that in the end we'll split. I don't want that to happen.

'I'm not shy of sex. I had a lot of blokes in my teens – used to go out drinking a lot and end up in bed with some fella. But I could never remember much about it afterwards and as I grew up a bit, I concentrated on quality rather than quantity!'

Degrees of Inhibition: Alcohol and Sex

There is a direct connection between difficulty with orgasm, alcohol and drugs. Although Haley says she doesn't drink as much as she used to, it rapidly becomes clear that she still manages to knock back quite a lot. In small quantities alcohol can release inhibition and this can be good for someone with problems of letting go sexually. Unfortunately, in larger quantities alcohol tends to fog sexual sensation, making it really difficult to conjure up anything at all. If you consider that men are actually made impotent by too much drink, it's not surprising that women have a non-orgasmic equivalent. Smoking too much pot and taking opiate drugs can also devastate sexual response.

KATE

Kate is 34. She's a social worker and has worked professionally for twelve years. She is slight and looks tired and drawn. Her clothes are colourless and when she speaks, her descriptions are halting. She has been in an on-off relationship with the same man for the past two years and prior to meeting him had had two serious love affairs, although she never actually lived with any of her lovers.

She never masturbated as a young woman, although she does recollect masturbating publicly in a room full of adults as a child of four.

'I didn't realise then that you shouldn't do this – it just happened without my thinking. But I remember my father looking at me, looking as though he liked what he saw and then telling me to stop. That night I was waiting in bed for him to say goodnight and I tried doing it again. He came in and saw me. This time I stopped as soon as he came in. But he didn't say anything. Just kissed me goodnight and put the light out. Somehow I must have got the message that there was something dangerous in doing it. Because I don't ever remember doing it again. I felt confused.'

It quickly becomes apparent that Kate is still confused. Ian, her boyfriend, refuses to make any permanent commitment to Kate, such as marriage, or even just moving in together. This hasn't stopped him from spending more time with her than ever.

'He's an old-fashioned guy. He expects me to be there to make supper for him and to be generally available. I know he occasionally goes out with other women, although he hasn't actually told me this. But if I ever breathe a word about the possibility of *my* dating someone else, he goes mad.

'I would quite like to marry him. But, at the moment, I do feel undervalued. He takes me for granted, an appendage of himself. He expects to be able to come round and spend a night with me whenever he feels like it. But he doesn't bother to turn up if he doesn't feel like it. That would be fair if the same rules applied equally to both of us. But apparently they don't.'

Kate's chronic lack of confidence has been enough to send her off to a counsellor for advice. And it is on that advice that she has decided to pursue an orgasm.

'I feel less than a woman not being able to climax,' she explains. 'I finally decided I was old enough to do something about it. I was pretty nervous about telling the counsellor my problems. I feel terrified about telling all of you. But she, the counsellor, recommended the group.'

Misbeliefs

One of the things that can happen in childhood is that we may hear or experience something which, because we don't fully understand it, we misunderstand. Literally, we form a misbelief. And whole chunks of life may be based on such misbeliefs. So if, like Kate, you've picked up some very mixed messages about the desirability of masturbating, you may believe this is a really bad thing to do. And if this somehow accidentally gets associated with the general experience of sex, it can result in inhibition. In other words, because you have the misbelief that sex is wrong, your unconscious stops you going too far – from having an orgasm.

THE PROBLEMS

FAKING

When Mary mentions she'd once faked orgasm with her husband, Haley confesses that she often did that with Len. 'Why did you stop?' she asks Mary. 'And how?'

'I'd done it with a previous boyfriend,' Mary explains. 'It hadn't helped anything and when I found myself faking during the early days with Bruce, I forced myself to stop short. I confessed. He was, and is, marvellous about my lack of orgasm. I'm the one who's fed up with it.'

'Why do you fake, Haley?' I ask.

'I don't want Len to feel he's not a success in bed. It's important to him to think of himself as a good lover.'

'But it's all right for you to go without a climax?'

'Yes – no. I don't know.'

'Has it occurred to you that by letting Len think you were satisfied by his methods of lovemaking you were *training* him to make love to you in the wrong way?'

This is a new idea for Haley. Having digested it, she then wants to know what she could do about it. 'Should I tell him I fake?'

'How often do you do it?' I ask.

'About one in four times we make love. Certainly not every time. Len knows I find it hard to climax. What he doesn't know is that I've only ever had an orgasm with him twice.'

Some counsellors believe that the only way to make a partnership work is by confessing to faking and starting again. I qualify that by taking into account the whole marriage or relationship and the depth to which faking is affecting it. In Haley and Len's case, owning up seemed unnecessary since the deception was a minor one. Rather than risk an upset, which might do more damage than good, it seemed preferable that she should wind down the faking so that eventually she could cut it out of their love life completely. Since Len was well aware that she *did* have orgasmic problems, this wasn't likely to make much difference to their marriage. At the same time, getting Len to take part in some of the exercises that constituted our homework each week would enable him (and Haley) to know more about what actually turned her on and would take some of the performance pressure off her.

FAKING ALL THE TIME

At a previous workshop to this, 26-year-old Ronnie confessed that she faked all the time with her boyfriend, that he had no idea she couldn't climax and that she had lied to him about her reasons for attending the group.

Ronnie was another woman with no self-confidence. She was pretty, petite and competent at her job but she had got used to Tom making all the decisions for her and she had also got used to him taking it for granted that he was doing her a big favour by his patronage. Ronnie had to do as she was told otherwise he would leave her. For two years Ronnie had done precisely that. But she turned out to be non-orgasmic, although she did try to masturbate and had on occasion asked Tom to do it for her. 'He was very reluctant, though, and did a very heavy job.'

During the six weeks of the course Ronnie developed in two ways. Firstly, she learned to masturbate to orgasm using a vibrator. Secondly, she realised through intense discussion with the group that her entire relationship with Tom (and not just the sex) was a poor one. With the support of the group, Ronnie took the decision to reveal all to Tom. When she did, his reaction was so aggressive and unsympathetic that Ronnie, after a two-week verbal battle, asked him to leave. She had managed to work out for herself that he was an unsuitable partner. The fake sex was, in this case, a reflection of the fake relationship.

Tom could have simmered down and, if he valued Ronnie, could have given thought to changing their life together. That was his option. He was unsuited to her character and personality. Part of her need to attend the group was in order to realise this.

The Group's Unconscious Needs

Every group has a life of its own. Some are cheerful and fun, others are angry and blaming. Some of it depends on the facilitator's frame of mind – the group I ran at the time I suffered a problem pregnancy was pretty disastrous. Some of it depends on the characters of the women taking part. Every individual comes to that group with her own unconscious needs. These may differ greatly from her neighbours. Yet even if they do, such can be the strength of group feeling that each woman can feel massively supported by the others, energised enough to make the necessary changes in her life. These needs unfold as the weeks of the group pass by.

CHILDHOOD SEXISM

Childhood sexism, that is, unconscious prejudice towards girls and boys, sexism that is (perhaps unconscious) prejudice towards girls and sometimes boys is nothing like as deep-seated as it was thirty years ago. Unfortunately, traces of it linger on. Some of this is because there are real sex differences (although surprisingly few). Some of this is because older parents have passed down inherited attitudes from *their* parents' generation. And some of this is because although we know we shouldn't be prejudiced, it nevertheless suits us to be so.

The problem with sexual discrimination is that it can be imperceptibly built into our lives and so we don't know it's there. If you grow up in a family that thinks girls should do the washing-up while the boys play ball outside, it's difficult to think outside that box.

Maggie is a particular victim of sexism in that her father discounted anything contributed by the women in his family. Only male opinion mattered. The result is that Maggie learned from her mother that the best way to cope with men, or indeed with any serious subject, is to keep away from them or retreat into childlike behaviour. This also explained why Maggie is so much more at ease in the company of women than in mixed groups.

'As a child I used to get on well with him,' she recalls. 'Then everything changed.' So today, if she feels at all threatened, even within the group, she retreats. She presses back on her seat as far as she can go before replying. She fiddles with her long hair like a schoolgirl and her voice rises to childlike levels. When she laughs, however, her voice becomes deep and rich, and when she's happy and excited, she sounds contralto. Her speech tones are a window to her anxieties.

But we are *all* victims of sexism – it's aimed not only at females. From the time we graduate beyond childhood, girls are expected to be passive and acquiescent, boys to take the initiative. This is especially relevant sexually. A young girl who is promiscuous is bad-mouthed by her mates; a boy, on the other hand, is thought of highly.

Even when it comes to the technicalities of sex, and in these enlightened times, a woman may still be expected to lie back and take what's on offer. An Irish woman, Liz, aged 23 and a mother of two, once told me, 'I've never really done very much in bed. I thought he'd know all about it. I mean he's supposed to do all that foreplay, isn't he?' Liz incidentally didn't read – never a magazine, newspaper or book. She suffered from a combination of a lack of imagination and of ignorance.

The conditioning can go deeper than the technicalities. 'I can't have orgasms with him,' said Margaret, aged 38 and married to a British Asian. 'But I honestly don't mind. He has a good time and I always feel good seeing him satisfied.'

As women we are often taught that it is wrong to feel pleasure and this can include sexual pleasure. Nobody actually sits down and tells us this but it is often implicit in the expectations that our nearest and dearest have of us. As wives, housekeepers and mothers we are usually asked to supply favourable conditions for the sensual enjoyment (eating, sleeping, hygiene, sex) of others. Even in an age when many men do help with cooking, shopping and household chores, it is still up to us to juggle all these needs at the back of the brain and make sure they are met somehow. There isn't a lot of time for ourselves.

Maggie, for example, during her teens always had to help with the washing-up. Her father and elder brother never did. They simply sat down and watched television. Even nowadays girls are often expected to help more with household chores than boys It is young children and men who are encouraged to enjoy. Not nearly so much women. Since we were once children, this breeds resentment. Some of us have excellent memories. So does our unconscious.

But sexism is not all one-sided. It works to the detriment of men too. Why should it be men who are expected to know their partner's sensual spots if she doesn't know them herself? And how can men be expected to know the right formula for turning on a woman if she doesn't know it about herself?

It is our responsibility as women to know our own bodies and how they function. When the function in question is sex and its dysfunction has the far-reaching ability to disrupt the lives of partners and children, it is sound common sense to do some personal research on our sensual responses.

Which means learning to masturbate. Masturbation is the act of stimulating the genitals (usually, specifically the clitoris) with the fingers or a vibrator or any safe object (that is, something unlikely to break and inflict injury) with the object of bringing on sexual arousal that may culminate in orgasm. And it's never too late to learn. Betty Dodson, the New York sex educator, once said that job satisfaction for her was teaching a 60-year-old woman to orgasm for the first time.

SEXUAL MYTHS

Both men and women suffer from the false idea that all women have the same sexual responses and that, as long as you carry out your foreplay strictly according to formula, you can't go wrong: if by some freak of chance your woman doesn't respond, it means that something is the matter with her. But just as our faces differ one from another, so too do our erotic responses; which means that to be successful in bed, firstly you need to know your own sensual responses (exactly what kind of touch makes you feel good and where), and then there is the tricky job of getting this valuable information across to your partner. But it can be done.

Perhaps the greatest myth about sexuality is that the 'right' way to climax is through intercourse and that any alternative way is immature, inferior, 'only for lesbians' (as Mary said) and unnatural. *The Hite Report* (1974) by Shere Hite was a ground-breaking account of women's sexuality based on 3,000 questionnaires filled in by women mostly from the New York area. In it, only 30 per cent of those women reported that they could have orgasm regularly through intercourse. However, 82 per cent of the same women said they could climax regularly by masturbation. Every other survey on the same subject since has produced the same statistics.

Women everywhere can feel confidence in waking up and realising that what seems to be the most 'natural' way of climaxing is *not* in the time-honoured missionary position under a bloke, but by masturbation: on your own, with your lover or by your lover, with or without penetration. When you take that sexological revelation and apply it to the bedroom routine, a whole lot of pressures fly out of the conjugal window.

Jan, on hearing this, realises 'that there's nothing wrong with me after all', which all of a sudden casts some light, or should I say blight, on her lover's behaviour. Kate, who had been feeling 'less of a woman, not to be able to climax', experiences a rush of self-confidence. Haley's reaction is 'so I'm not frigid'.

SELF-CONFIDENCE

A continual theme running through everyone's story in the groups is of feeling undervalued, ineffectual, and lacking in self-esteem and self-confidence. Maggie, on mulling over her belittling upbringing, begins to understand how her confidence had not only been undermined but had never been allowed to develop. 'At least I do sometimes argue with Dad,' she says thoughtfully, 'and I *was* able to get out – to leave. That was a positive thing to do. But then I think of my mother, who can't leave. She just sits there, retreating into herself, never speaking unless she's spoken to. He only talks to her if he wants something done.

'The trouble is,' she continues, 'I don't know how to become effective. I boil up with rage in an argument but when I open my mouth to speak, anything I say sounds silly. It's better if I keep quiet. I didn't really want Joe to leave me two years ago but there didn't seem to be anything to say that would be important enough to persuade him to stay. He didn't leave me because he disliked living with me; he went because he was offered a good job in India.'

Later in the training (weeks two and three), we will do an exercise that teaches us how to become more assertive. Today, however, we will try something to help build up Maggie's self-knowledge and subsequently her self-esteem.

Building Self-Esteem

- Swot up on topics you know come up regularly with friends and family. This is so you have the facts at your fingertips if it comes to an argument.
- Work out clear lines of argument in advance so that you can steer the conversation.
- Rehearse in front of a mirror.
- Rehearse with a female friend – do a trial run or two.

If you know what you are talking about you will have faith in yourself during a discussion. Once you have this faith you will find it easier to pursue whatever line you feel strongly about and to stick to your guns. A large part of an argument is discussion – regardless of who is right or wrong. So just stick with the discussion – it's half the battle.

It's a long haul. It takes most of us the first twenty or thirty years of our life to become effective in verbal battle. Maggie has the disadvantage of having to build up confidence at the age of 26 instead of starting in babyhood. But it can be done. And it shouldn't take her too long since she has already acquired a lot of the basic skills and facts. But it *is* hard work and we all of us have to learn it.

What is the relevance of all this to sexuality? Your level of self-confidence as a woman is related to your determination to experience orgasm. Just as Maggie gathers facts together so that she is familiar with her arguments and can use them effectively, so too do we need to know the facts about our sensuality and sexuality. This building up of confidence helps get us past an orgasm block. Once past the block, self-confidence increases more rapidly and we become more skilled at climaxing.

Of course, not all women are 'put down' as females, nor do they all have the same lack of confidence. But undermining women's sexuality is insidious. Take, for example, menstruation – something that affects every single fertile woman on the planet (about half the population, in other words). There has only ever been one major book on the psychology of menstruation (*The Wise Wound* by Peter Redgrove and Penelope Shuttle, 1974); there has been virtually no current thought given to the social effects menstruation has on a family, although Dr Katherina Dalton did her utmost in the 1960s to raise our consciousness; it's only recently that we have gained any notion of why some of us have more or less blood loss; and it's only since people like me linked monthly hormone fluctuation with mood that it dawned on us this might radically affect the female experience of love-making and orgasm. Yet we women make up half the human race.

In history, female sexuality hasn't counted for much. We have been valued for territory or money that might be brought in marriage or for our labouring and mothering skills, and certainly as sex objects for the pleasure of others. But we are only just, in the 21st century, being looked on as sexual beings in our own right.

VALUING MASTURBATION

One of the findings of running sexuality groups over the years is that there is a huge common denominator among the women attending – one that is pretty obvious even from only reading up to this point. That is that most women who are pre-orgasmic suffer from real difficulties with confidence. Job satisfaction for *me* is seeing each individual's confidence grow as the weeks of the group progress. There are some women who gain it as a *result* of learning to climax while there are others for whom valuing themselves goes hand-in-hand with *getting to know* that prize of sexuality, self-pleasuring.

Masturbation is the act of stimulating the genitals (usually specifically the clitoris) with the fingers, a vibrator or any safe object (something unlikely to break and inflict injury) with the object of bringing sexual arousal that may culminate in orgasm.

Masturbation is a delightful, fulfilling and restoring experience in its own right. It's a healer, an energy giver, an alleviator of tension, a gift of self-pleasure and it *can* be an ecstatic experience.

But some people remain worried and suspicious of masturbation. 'Are you saying that it would be all right never to have an orgasm during intercourse?' asked Katherine – an isolated housewife who lived in some unfriendly suburbs.

My answer to her was that it doesn't matter in the slightest if you fail to orgasm through penis–vagina friction only. What does matter is that you should be able to orgasm in *some* way together. As well as being a sexual marvel in its own right, masturbation can also be used as a major part of lovemaking so that it allows an expression of love between two people.

Many people equate making love with being in love and being loved, and to them it is important to reach orgasm when having sex together. But I would reiterate that as long as orgasm does happen, I don't think it matters at all whether it's by intercourse, or masturbation during intercourse, by mutual masturbation or by individual masturbation while in each other's company. What does matter is that you are doing something loving together which gives you sexual happiness.

I used to broadcast on an English radio programme about women's sexuality and answer listeners' phone calls on sex problems. One sad and depressed woman in her late fifties described a marriage of thirty years that had been totally without orgasm for her. The relationship had deteriorated to the point where the couple now had very little contact with each other at all socially, and none whatsoever sexually. Indeed, Mrs X and her husband had separate bedrooms. 'What is the use', this worn-down voice asked, 'of learning to masturbate? It's far too late for it to be any good to my husband.'

'Blow your husband,' was my immediate indignant response. 'What about yourself?' Mrs X had had a lifetime of thinking her sexuality was something that existed simply for marriage. The thought that it was something existing primarily for *her* was very new. The idea that she, as a person, was important and that her sexuality reflected that importance was totally unfamiliar.

At least she rang off, promising to try.

My outrage at Mrs X's desire to parcel herself away in celibacy until she conveniently departed this life was picked up by another listener in the same age bracket. This second woman had also endured a miserable married life. But three years ago her husband had died. To begin with she had forced herself to be outgoing, to cope with his absence. But she rapidly discovered that life was much more fun than she'd ever given it credit for. As well as making friends, she'd bought a vibrator and had begun to have orgasms. 'I want to reassure Mrs X,' she said, 'that 57 is not the end of the line and that there's plenty to live for. My advice is to start now and make the most of the short time that's left.'

There has been such an outpouring of sexual information during the past few decades that it is unlikely any woman today hasn't at least heard of masturbation and vibrators. But my reason for including these two stories is to illustrate these women's attitudes to life. Each woman had specific *expectations*, which had literally shaped their sex lives. And yet the second woman had discovered, by experimentation, the joy of self-pleasure and her life had changed. By doing so she also changed her expectations.

I am not suggesting we would be better off without partners. But I am saying we all have the means within ourselves to be sexually fulfilled.

Biologically, part of orgasm's original function was probably to encourage sexual encounters between men and women for the purpose of procreation. But I suspect the delight of climax was given to both sexes to *keep them happy*, not just to make babies. After all, we don't *need* female orgasm to procreate. What do we need it for? I think climax was evolved not just as a reward for copulation but also as a safeguard against destructive aggression. It operates by relaxing our bodies when otherwise they might be subject to constant tension. Thus it has been a biological means of making us easier to live with. And masturbation, as a prime means of experiencing orgasm, is a way of ensuring our survival through fostering happy communal strength, preventing our species from being dissipated and disrupted through built-up tension and anger.

MYTHS OF MASTURBATION

Contrary to repressive folklore, masturbation does not make you go blind, deaf, catch flu, send you insane or kill you. The Victorian idea that each teaspoon of lost semen weakened a man equivalent to a lost pint of blood is without any basis, and for women, the suggestion that masturbation leads to concupiscence (unbridled lust) and nymphomania is also untrue. The last belief, however, is interesting in that, in earlier times, it may have been women with a higher sex drive who dared to take these masturbation 'risks'; the same women may also have been the most active ones with sexual partners, and therefore would have been most open to sexual innuendo and slander.

SECOND-HAND SATISFACTION

Mary has been fascinated by something Haley said about her husband's orgasms.

Haley: 'A lot of the time I've been satisfied by him coming.'

Mary: 'How do you mean?'

Haley: 'Well, he's had such obvious pleasure from his climax and he's been so loving to me as a result of it, that I've felt a pleasure and satisfaction through him even though I myself don't technically come.'

Me: 'That's fine as long as you're happy with it. Pretty obviously, though, you're not or you wouldn't be here.'

Haley: 'I don't seem to be any more. Why do you think that is?'

Me: 'It can be lovely enjoying someone else's orgasm but not as a full-time occupation. And it's very much part of the passive wife–active husband syndrome, that "the only right and proper way to be a sexual woman is through your partner". I don't think so! That's another sex myth.'

ORGASM MYTHS

Maxie: 'I thought that the ideal was for you both to have an orgasm simultaneously and as a result of this, experience a *marvellous feeling of oneness* [said in a funny voice].'

Me: 'Like so many sexual happenings it *can* be great but the minute you start turning orgasms into "ideals" and "goals" you alter the experience with the potential to ruin it. I've had simultaneous orgasms, which have been lovely but leave me feeling flat afterwards. I've also had orgasms first, then gone on making love with my man until he has climaxed, which have been much better. It depends entirely on your feelings at the time.'

'SELFISHNESS' OF ORGASM

Haley: 'What about *becoming one*? It sounds like a religious high spot.'

Me: 'As I've said, there's no room in a climax for thoughts of others. You can't do it. Orgasm is a completely self-absorbed experience, which focuses totally upon the sensual feelings in only *your* brain and *your* body. I'm not talking about the lead-up to orgasm but the experience itself. When you climax you are far out in your head, going through wave after mental wave. You are not aware, while this is actually going on, of any of your partner's thought processes or of what he is experiencing. That's why orgasm has been termed a "little death". In fact, if you do suddenly tune into your partner, you'll find your climax suddenly loses strength and sensation.'

Haley: 'But you do get a feeling of togetherness. I've felt that with Len.'

Me: 'Afterwards, of course you do. You're as close and loving as two people can be and you've just shared a beautiful experience. When you're having sex with someone you love, it's about the ultimate in togetherness. But you can get those warm, shared feelings however you manage to bring on the climax. You don't have to have intercourse to get them. You are *never* two people who become one. There are always two people, having two experiences, albeit at the *same* time.'

AUTOMATIC SWITCH-OFF

Kate: 'I get to a certain point of excitement and then something goes dead. Something inside my head switches off and stops me feeling sexy.'

Me: 'You need to find what it is that's making you do that. It could be childhood conditioning about sex being "dirty", or a fear of losing control, or an unconscious need to punish yourself, or a lack of sensual knowledge about yourself. If you are talking about lovemaking with a partner, it may be that unconsciously you resent him or even that you are secretly distrustful of all males. It might simply be that you need to be more determined and carry on for far longer than you imagine is necessary.'

I don't go into a long analysis of each person's subconscious fears even though, here, I have a strong idea of what is checking Kate's sexual response. The emphasis is on the women doing the thinking and making the connections for themselves, not in having the answers conveniently provided. After talking briefly about such fears at this first meeting, most women leave looking extremely thoughtful. Part of their homework is to keep a diary during the course, which can prove invaluable for thinking back into the past and working out actions and motivations.

THE HOMEWORK

WEEK ONE HOMEWORK

Part of the commitment to the six-week group course is to agree to do homework. This involves doing something every single day of the week for one hour only. I say only but it is actually quite difficult to carve a separate hour a day out of busy lives. Nevertheless, if you want to improve your sensual awareness you need to organise it. As my mother would say, 'It's for your own good'. The homework for Week One includes bio-energetic exercises designed to re-awaken the energy flow around the pelvic area and to teach us how to generate tension there. First come the exercises, then the schedule.

THE EXERCISES

RELAXATION VERSUS TENSION

The advice given for years by GPs faced with female patients complaining of lack of orgasm has been to relax. And although feeling relaxed when beginning to make love can be nice, it is not essential. What is essential, though, is that when you approach climax the pelvic area is tensed. It is by *building up* tension and therefore energy that a reflex action – like a sneeze – occurs, which releases that energy. And the name of this reflex? Orgasm. So, if you consciously relax when hoping for a climax you are doing yourself a great disservice.

Rather, exaggerate that tension, arch your back, push your pelvis up into the air, breathe in short breaths, tense your knees and thighs, wriggle and jiggle your genitals.

BIO-ENERGETIC PELVIC EXERCISES

Bio-energetics is a therapy that uses an understanding of the body to heal the problems of the mind. By direct bodywork using these exercises, muscular tension can be dissolved, leaving an increased level of physical and mental wellbeing. If you have any back problems, attempt the pelvic lift and pelvic rock with extreme care. If in doubt, leave them out, although most people with back pain find the exercises alleviate it.

1. Relaxation exercise

- Lie flat on your back on the floor (not a bed).
- Breathe in slowly through your nose and out through your mouth. As you continue it may help to let the breath out with a slight exaggeration (eg. say 'her' on the out-breath).
- After a couple of minutes start noticing, while you continue with the breathing, which parts of your body remain tense. Try consciously to relax them. Begin at the tip of the right foot and work your way up the right leg, relaxing any part of it that may be tense.
- When you reach the top, go back down to the left foot and come up that leg.
- Once you reach the abdomen, work your way up to your neck, relaxing as you go along.
- Then relax the right arm.
- Next the left arm…
- Ending with the neck and the head.

A good way to relax tense spots is to exaggerate that tension for a minute, by clenching the muscle then letting go. So, tense then let go all the way up the body as just described. Spend fifteen minutes on this.

When you have finished the exercise (and after any other which involves lying on your back), make sure you do not sit up immediately but take your time about it. In order to avoid letting the blood rush unpleasantly from your head, don't sit up with a jerk but rather roll over on to your stomach and get up while facing the ground. This is a calmer and more peaceful method by which to rise.

2. Grounding

- Stand with your feet firmly about 45 cm (18 inches) apart, with your toes pointing in towards each other and your knees slightly bent, fists pressing into your back, just above your waist. Don't let up on this heel pressing. It helps to imagine that energy is flowing up from the earth through your feet and legs the harder you press down.

- Hold this stance for as long as your neck and legs can bear it (breathing as described at the beginning of the grounding exercise) and when the time comes to stand up straight, do so on an out-breath.

- Once up, on the out-breath let the top half of your body fall forward so that the tips of your hands are nearly touching the ground. And hold this, while grounding those heels constantly.

- After a couple of minutes, stand straight and relax. You should, after carrying out the exercise a couple of times, start to feel a vibration in the tops of your legs. When you begin to be aware of this, you know the exercise has worked. The vibration signals the release of the energy flow.

3. Pelvic lift

- Lying on your back, draw up your knees so that your feet are squarely on the ground. Keep your arms by your sides, palms down.

- Push up your bottom and arch your back so that they are right off the ground. Your body should only be touching the ground at the feet and from the shoulders upwards. You are actually resting on the shoulders. Hold this position for a couple of minutes, then bring your bottom down again.

4. Pelvic rock

- Lying on your back, palms down and legs flat, on an in-breath arch your back (keeping your bottom on the ground) and let your pelvis fall away from the direction of your head.
- On an out-breath, press your spine to the ground and pull your pelvis towards the direction of your head.
- By doing these two movements on the in–out of each breath you will be aware that you are rocking your pelvis backwards and forwards.

5. Squatting

- This involves squatting on the ground bushwhacker-style, with your arms inside your legs and your heels on the floor. Since most of us are not rubber-limbed contortionists it may be advisable to cheat at this exercise (to begin with) by putting a book beneath your heels (preferably a large one!). Hold on to somebody if you need to keep your balance. The object is to open up and relax the genital area while maintaining rhythmical breathing. Do this exercise for three minutes.

6. Pelvic circling

- Stand and move your hips in a circle forward, side, back, side, around and around as though you are a hula dancer. Become aware of how you are breathing and ensure that, as with all the other exercises, you breathe evenly and rhythmically while you circle. Do this in first one direction, then the other.

THE HOMEWORK DAILY SCHEDULE – WEEK ONE

Aim at doing about one hour a day.

Day 1: Get comfortable with yourself and your body. Take a bath, soap yourself slowly and caressingly, dry yourself and rub cream or lotion into your skin. If you don't have exclusive access to a bathroom, just do the self-massage in your bedroom. Sit or lie on a towel to prevent the lotion or cream from staining. Notice the different textures of skin and muscle. Take your time in caressing yourself. Enjoy yourself and get to know your body.

Day 2: 'Talk' your way through your body in front of a mirror. Note down your feelings about yourself in a diary.

Day 3: Spend today concentrating on the relaxation and bio-energetic exercises.

Day 4: Write your diary. The focus here is on anything you are noting about your body. This may be about how it feels when you touch it, what its texture is like. Or it may be about your feelings and experience of being in the group. Anything goes if it's focusing on your sensuality. Repeat the breathing and bio-energetic exercises.

Day 5: Same as Day 1.

Day 6: Spend an hour indulging yourself, doing *anything* you like. Play music, dance, write your diary and focus on anything you want to discuss at the group tomorrow. It's important to spend an hour doing *exactly what you want* and *not* what anyone else wants you to do.

If you can find the time, it's a good idea to try to practise the relaxation and bio-energetic exercises every day – but it's not essential.

ADDITIONAL READING

Great Sex Guide by Anne Hooper (Dorling Kindersley, 1995). A small book about sexual energy.

Total Orgasm by Jack Lee Rosenberg (Wildwood House, 1974). This is still the best book on the subject of bio-energetics and sex but sadly it is out of print. Second-hand copies can be bought from Amazon and AbeBooks online, and it may be available in some public libraries.

Chapter 2

WEEK TWO

Everyone looks happier. Kate has washed her hair and is wearing a very cool designer outfit. Haley wears a dashing combination of soft sweater and slash-red lipstick. Maggie has brushed out her hair instead of pulling it back into a severe knot. Mary has blossomed in a full-length emerald green smock and Maxie looks as immaculate as before. Jan is sporting a very cut-away tracksuit.

In case you think these comments on appearance are pure trivia, they do in fact have meaning. You can gauge people's progress in the group and how good they are feeling about themselves from the care they take of their looks. There's a direct connection between outer appearance and inner wellbeing.

TALKING ABOUT THE HOMEWORK

HALEY

Haley is feeling particularly smug and starts talking about her experiences as soon as we've arrived. Len has worked on a late shift most of this week so Haley has had clear time in which to practise her homework without interruption.

'All that bathing and stroking. I've felt sexier and sexier. Last night, when we could do anything we wanted to please ourselves, was great. I lay down naked on the rug in the living room listening to the most emotional music I could find. Fantastic.'

MARY

Mary isn't so enthusiastic. 'It's impossible to make so much time every night. That routine simply isn't designed for busy housewives.'

Groans from me since it is precisely to fit in with housewives that we've tried to plan the homework. I explain. 'The whole point is that we don't normally spend enough time on ourselves. Therefore we've *got* to be more selfish. We've *got* to make time for ourselves. That way we begin to value ourselves more.'

We go into the practicalities of Mary's time. During the day it is obviously impossible to find an hour to set aside since the children are very active. But the evening has distinct possibilities. 'Bruce expects me to be with him at night,' she says.

I get heavy. I've discovered, from letting the homework ride in past groups, that the course doesn't work if the homework isn't adhered to faithfully. The women have to understand how important it is and *must* find this time to spend on themselves.

Mary reluctantly sees the sense in this. 'But on the nights I did do it,' she continues, 'I felt funny. I kept thinking Bruce would come into the bedroom and I didn't want him to interrupt.'

'Lock the door,' we advise. 'It's the best way of knowing that no one is going to walk in.'

'There isn't a lock.'

'Then go out and buy a bolt. They're easy to fit.'

Mary subsides in dubious contemplation. 'Can I really lock Bruce out?'

'Yes, provided you explain exactly why, provided that he understands.'

'Um, maybe I will.'

KATE

Kate is sparkling with colour and confidence. 'I had things out with Ian at the weekend. It was a very hard and depressing thing to have to do. Especially when he said he had better move back into his own place. But instead of giving in, like I've always done in the past, I stuck to my guns. I felt awful seeing him go. I'd rather he'd said, "Let's get married and live happily ever after." But he didn't. And I can see that *I've* got to decide about *my* life. I'm convinced that I've done the right thing. I'm feeling really good about being so decisive.

'And it's changed my behaviour at work. I haven't been forceful enough previously and people mess me around because of it. But this week they haven't been allowed to. I've been clear and cool and I've insisted on having things done my own way. At an especially ferocious staff meeting today I stuck to the point I was making instead of giving way. I left it with a lot more respect for myself.'

Kate's inner self appears to be reacting to her new outer behaviour. In the past Kate has had mild orgasms in dreams. Now she relates a new dream she had two nights ago. 'I woke up to find my vagina contracting violently. I think it was an orgasm but it was quite different from any of the others. It was so strong it was shaking my entire body.'

Kate is also getting very active responses when she does the bio-energetic exercises. 'My vagina contracts. It makes gasping noises and I'm getting tingling feelings.'

Stimulation Research

Researchers at New York University carried out an experiment where they wired up equal numbers of men and women to record their physiological sexual responses.

When the people taking part were given erotic literature to read, all the men admitted to being turned on by it, which the monitoring apparatus confirmed. However, only half the women admitted to being excited by their reading *although the apparatus showed that they all were*. One conclusion to be drawn from the experiment is that many women are not able to identify or to tell the truth about their own feelings or arousal. So although many women deny being affected by erotica in the same way that men are, it now seems possible they are unaware or actually suppress their response.

MAGGIE
Maggie is far too quiet and I suspect she hasn't done as much of the homework as she ought. She lives alone now and has

no boyfriend, so everything she does is very decidedly for herself. But she's keen-eyed as she listens to the others.

JAN

Jan has had negative reactions on looking at her body nude in front of a mirror. This is strange, since she has beautiful skin and suppleness. Fortunately, the others tell her so.

Jan's boyfriend has felt very threatened by her coming to the course even though she appears to be doing it strictly for his benefit. She tells us more about him – the more she describes him, the worse he sounds.

'I'm not surprised you can't have orgasms with such a bully,' Mary echoes our thoughts. 'He sounds awful.'

He *is* a bully. He threatens her psychologically by telling her she's inefficient as a mother, can't be relied on and that if she doesn't watch out, he'll have her son, Will, taken away from her and put into care. He bashes her for the slightest step out of line – that is, what *he* considers to be out of line, which usually coincides with her having an opinion which differs from his. He lives off her money and contributes nothing to the household, either financially, practically or emotionally.

'Why do you stay with him?' asks Kate, in a daze.

Jan looks helpless. 'He's so attractive. I can't imagine ever wanting to go to bed with anyone else.'

'But he's ghastly,' everyone groans. 'You don't need him.'

Jan is thoughtful for the rest of the session. When we describe the YES/NO exercise, which is part of next week's homework (see the end of this chapter), she looks particularly contemplative.

MAXIE

Maxie too is quiet. She doesn't say a word while anyone else speaks but when specifically called on for an opinion, talks volubly. Maxie has been thinking about the men in her life and she's not happy with them. She's also begun to understand how basically ignorant she is about sex. 'I didn't know, till last week, that I might masturbate,' she tells us. 'And I still don't understand about the clitoris.'

Clitoris

The clitoris is an organ unique to women. It serves to both build up and to release sexual energy. It has no other purpose.

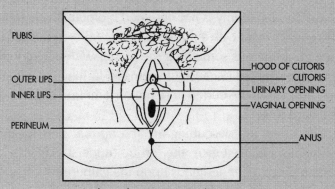

Vulva—the outer sex organs

All human embryos up to the sixth week of conception possess this genital bud of tissue and nerve endings. It is only after the sixth week, in those children destined to be boys, that the hormone testosterone sets to work and develops the clitoris into what eventually becomes the penis, a larger organ, which serves to void urine in addition to its sexual role. The clitoris works via stimulation. By stimulating the clitoris, by rubbing, stroking and caressing it, female sexual sensation is generated.

During the second group meeting we talk about the gaps in sex education for girls. Even today, few biology textbooks mention the clitoris. Most of them concentrate on the baby-making functions of sex. Most of the diagrams showing penis–vagina penetration depict the penis a million miles away from the clitoris. Fortunately, there are several sex manuals available, sensitive enough to be read by youngsters, that do show the clitoris.

Our clitoral anatomy is not designed biologically to come into easy contact with a thrusting penis. All six women say they think there is something the matter with where their clitoris is situated because 'it seems so far back', 'so high up', 'it seems to be buried underneath a mound of flesh' or 'it's hard to get at'.

What they are describing are the *normal* sites for this estimable organ. Once the group understands this a certain air of relief descends upon the gathering.

CLITORAL STIMULATION DURING INTERCOURSE

'But that means it can be very difficult to come during intercourse?' says Maxie.

'That's right. Unless of course you use some other kind of stimulation at the same time.'

'What kind of stimulation?' she asks.

'A finger to touch your clitoris while you're making love. Either your own finger or your partner's. And if fingers don't work, you can try a vibrator.'

Jan owns a vibrator, though none of the others do. 'It must be difficult to have the guts to take your vibrator to bed with you,' she says doubtfully. 'Doesn't your man think it's a put-down?'

'Try it and see. It can work very well. He may love it. He'll get some of the good vibrations too. Why not make sure that he does?'

SELF-IMAGE

One of the exercises in the homework last week was to look at ourselves naked in front of a mirror. Everyone, with the exception of Kate, disliked their nude bodies. There were resolutions to go on a diet, take more exercise and join a slimming club.

Why did they all think so poorly of themselves? Because none of them looked like a classic pin-up in the nude. It had never occurred to any of them just how unrealistic the currently fashionable female figure is. Today's ideal is Size 0, the uber-slim, the girl who, when she turns sideways, isn't there. Finally there is a public move against such body masochism.

The Media Nude

She's an image, an invention of the media, someone whose real curves are altered and 'enhanced' by a computer much of the time. Every time we see these unreal women sparkling at us from the pages of a fashion magazine, we are being conditioned to think this is the feminine ideal. Yet, if you look back through the history of fashion, you can see a variety of figures, which, at one time or another, were all the ideal.

In mediaeval days it was thought beautiful and desirable to look pregnant. In Elizabethan days you were all the rage if you had square shoulders. Nowadays, in Mediterranean countries, large-bellied women are considered attractive, while Latin Americans adore a large derrière. Look at J-Lo, who has insured her gorgeous behind for large sums of money!

Skinny North Europeans, on holiday, can often feel very unvoluptuous when surrounded by well-rounded women who in their own culture appear beautiful. What I'm trying to say is that we are as beautiful as we feel, not as the media dictates. Kate agrees. She is flat-chested and likes looking that way. But no one else in the group is satisfied with the way they look.

How are these six women feeling about coming to the group?

Maggie, who has remained mute so far, looks on the point of tears when she says how very supported she felt last week when everyone tried to think up ways to help her become more effective in discussion. It is quiet, pale Maggie who blossoms in the next part of the evening when we go on to learn how to do a body massage together.

MASSAGE

Everyone has brought a towel this week and a bottle of sweet-smelling massage oil. Good massage oil is expensive to buy but you can make your own quite cheaply by scenting baby oil with perfume. I personally have always used suntan oil.

'Let's get it over and done with,' says Kate, preparing for an ordeal. Maggie is rooted to her seat, paralysed with fright. But no one needs to move yet because I do a demonstration first. At some workshops, Jo takes her clothes off and I massage her. At others, I undress and she massages me. Either way, we've both learned we must be relaxed about being naked in front of a new group. That way, when it comes to their turn to be nude, it doesn't have to seem such a big step for them.

Once I have demonstrated the massage strokes I become matter of fact and efficient. 'OK, take a partner. Kate with Haley, Mary with Maggie, Maxie with Jan.' When they see there is no way they're going to get out of this, they reluctantly take off their clothes.

But once their partner's warm hands slide firmly along their oiled backs the reluctance disappears. Now that they have been forced to have this experience there is no alternative but to lie back and enjoy it. And enjoy it they do. The massage is transforming. They love it. They shed their inhibitions. They understand how daft it is to keep their pants on when they get so ridiculously in the way. They sit up afterwards totally unconcerned about their nudity. The women with lovers want to get back home and try the strokes out on them. Sometimes they feel so strongly about massage that at the end of the course they start their own massage workshop. Massage is a fantastic vehicle for change.

The greatest change tonight is in Maggie. She's no longer the tired little girl. Her usually childlike voice rings with a new decisiveness.

There have been two women at previous groups whose lives have literally been transformed by massage. Lily was a 20-year-old German girl who was a student in the United Kingdom. She was so deep in depression she nearly committed suicide. She hadn't been near a man for two years because she was in despair at never being able to experience a climax. She had become convinced there was no room in the world for her any longer, that she was a sexual and emotional misfit, and she used to sit alone in her room, night after night, crying.

The day we did the massage with her group had been an especially bad day for her. (Earlier she had been on the phone to Jo telling her that life wasn't worth living.) But that same evening, during the massage, she discovered firstly that she could actually tolerate someone touching her and secondly that the touch felt so good she felt hopeful again.

During the weeks that followed she changed drastically. She bought herself new clothes, looked ten times healthier, lost her depression and shortly afterwards stopped going to the psychiatrist she'd been seeing for years. She went on to use a vibrator and never looked back.

Heather was in another group. She was a 36-year-old South African who'd lived in this country since she was 20. She was suffering from a depression so stultifying she could hardly speak. She'd been attending group psychotherapy and subsequently one-to-one therapy for seven years. She lived on her own, never read, never watched television and never went out, except to her job. She sat in her one room, thinking and doing nothing, year after year. Her job as a clerk in the post office required nothing in the way of talent or initiative and therefore she was able to carry it out like a robot. Her psychotherapist had suggested she should join our group.

Heather was extremely reluctant to take part in the massage; she couldn't see that there was any point to it and was terrified we would think her body was unattractive. 'I've got bad spots,' she told us.

Her spots turned out to be only in her mind. Her first massage made her feel wonderful. In the space of half an hour she became amazingly relaxed. By the next meeting she had bought and tried out a vibrator.

'It blew the top of my head off,' she said simply.

Being naked in a group is an amazing leveller. It allows you to see that you are normal. Your lumps and bumps are much the same as anyone else's. Heather found out she was no different to the others and she felt much better for the discovery.

When Heather left the course she was still subject to fits of depression but she had also acquired hope. We last heard that she was more assertive and self-confident, and that she was trying to change her job towards something more creative.

So, what is the point of massage? First of all, it is a wonderful sensual experience. Secondly, it forces us to accept pleasure focused solely on ourselves and not on anyone else. It provides one of the rare times when all other demands for our attention fade into the background as we enjoy sensuality focused on us alone. One of the most important lessons we can learn is to accept and enjoy that sensuality.

MASSAGE WITH PARTNERS

Massage also establishes new channels of communication with loving partners. (One type of massage is the basis of the sex therapy exercises popularised by the US sex researchers Masters and Johnson and practised in sex therapy clinics around the world.) Often women, who have found it hard in pre-orgasmic homework to touch and stroke themselves, suddenly understand what they've been aiming at when they have a massage session later with their husband or lover.

Each lover gains valuable information about their partner's body. Just as some of us are ticklish on the feet and others are not, so too other zones of our body are either sensual or non-sensual.

I have a deliciously sexy feeling when I'm touched down the side of my body from the armpit to the hips. Jo, on the other hand, finds her good sensations are focused directly on her neck and shoulders.

It's important to know these sensual facts about ourselves, important to know the erotic geography of our own bodies. If we are familiar with these erogenous zones it will be all the better for getting the information across to our partners. And when he or she has received the information that we have become able to transmit, he or she will consequently be all the better skilled at pleasing us.

A massage in the group is usually such fun that we find it a glowing finale to the second evening together. In a haze of goodwill, we leave each other's bodies and, fortified by touch, plunge back into the outside world.

AN EXPERIENCE OF MASSAGE

My local wise man was practised in massage. I was anxious to experience at first hand the ecstasies he described, so I encouraged him to invite me round.

His flat has one immense room, furnished with low-lying cushions, mattresses and Japanese-style tables. In spite of the sheer area, it is hot – most conducive to taking one's clothes off.

Soft, melodious Japanese music is played and I am invited to lie down on my stomach, on a thin mattress on the floor. He is wearing Eastern whites, a soft, loose white cotton top, and tie-over white cotton trousers with no fly. It's interesting how he's managed to create such an atmosphere of relaxation and luxury in a basic one-room apartment – there's such simplicity.

I am offered a choice of oils, perfumed with separate fragrances. I choose the least lurid and softest scented. I find it hard to undress in front of someone I don't know intimately, but try to make as if I'm at the doctor's so that the scene feels impersonal. But it isn't. Eventually naked, I hurry to lie face down on the floor.

His hands are warm, and he rubs the oil into them before transferring it to my body. 'Try deep breathing,' he suggests. 'Concentrate on making your mind go blank.' I obey. It isn't hard to relax. And apart from explaining what he is going to do, he dislikes talking. He says it distracts him from the attention he is focusing on me. The lights are dim, and even though I'm tense, it's already good to feel so concentrated on.

He is very experienced at massage and to my untrained body very good. He not only knows a great variety of hand movements but he achieves a variety of sensations by using three different layers of pressure. So what starts off as a slippery glide across the skin deepens into a tension loosener, which eventually becomes a precise burning feeling as if he were running a long fingernail down inside my flesh. But he isn't – he's just using the deepest pressure of all!

He is aware of my tensions, where they are reflected and at what kind of body layer they can be skilfully manipulated. Most important of all, he tunes in mentally to what my body requirements seem to be, and almost telepathically holds me just right.

At no time do I feel irritated, uncomfortable or in any way uneasy. He makes a point of never taking his touch from me, even when he is applying extra oil, or having a rest.

It's when you are touched so confidently and so intimately that you become clearly awake to the lack of touch you experience every day. I never want him to stop, never want him to take his hands off me.

And when, after a timeless period, he decides he has done enough and does stop, I simply refuse to move, lying there, still ecstatic.

It must be amusing for him, and maybe flattering too, to see what a powerful effect he has provoked. Certainly I arouse him. It must be virtually impossible to touch a woman with every skill imaginable, to see her physical reactions and hear her verbal ones, without becoming just a little aroused yourself.

When early on he massages down my arms, culminating in deep palm-to-palm hand movements, his touch is startlingly warm and sensual. I experience such powerful surges of love and affection that I don't want him to let go of my hand.

It is the friendliest, most loving physical sensation I have ever known outside touch in a love affair. I feel so good and happy just from this that I wish everybody could have a massage every day of their life!

I learn an immense amount about myself. I hadn't realised how much I needed touch and attention. I could do anything if I were free to give and receive that kind of attention every single day!

It isn't just the physical sensation he engenders in me. It is the mental rapport, where I, with my physical reactions, lead him on to creating more and better stimulation so that I, in my turn, again become ecstatic, not just in the body but in the mind. The proof of this marvellous positive energy he has drawn out of me is my active desire to make him as happy as he's made me. So that when he finally finishes the massage and we sit cross-legged on the floor drinking orange juice (after such an intimate experience, there are no inhibitions about being naked!), I suggest I should massage him.

I am a little nervous in case my unsure touch should be an anti-climax after the mass of sensation he's provoked between us, but he is pleased at the suggestion. I go to work. It is quite amazing to know that you are provoking such feelings of sensual delight.

And the more I tune in to him and the pleasures he is receiving, the more daring I feel.

I dare to concentrate on the erogenous zones; I dare to massage his bottom with confidence. (It's quite daunting faced with a strange bottom to know just how intimate you can and ought to be...)

His bottom turns out to be the most erogenous zone of all, so that I can touch him there, anywhere, firmly, upwards, downwards, make my hands swim in circles, pull my fingertips deliberately over him, and whatever I do, he reacts strongly and sexually.

It's almost frightening, observing the kind of power I momentarily hold over this man. And learning from earlier reactions, I know that having aroused him there, the rest of his body is stretching out, receptive to similar sensuality... If after half an hour I hadn't become so tired, I would happily have gone on for ever.

No, we didn't make love. It could have happened so easily after those hours of perfect intimacy. But I had inhibitions about that. Soon afterwards, on another occasion, I did teach my lover the things that my wise man had gently introduced me to. And although neither of us actually meant to turn it into a lovemaking session, that is what it became. By the end of one hour of massage, we were both so aroused we made some of the most sensual love that he and I have ever made together.

HOW TO DO A MASSAGE

Preparing a massage means creating a relaxed and receptive mood for the person you are massaging. The sex of your partner is irrelevant to the details of the eroto-fantasy you propose to conjure in his/her senses, so whether your lover is male or female, the sensual framework remains the same.

THE RULES
Dim the lights, or light a candle, burn a sweet-smelling joss stick or scented candle, make sure that you have a compilation of soft and harmonious music on the sound system, or a peaceful silence (turn off your mobile phone), and above all keep the room as warm as possible. If necessary, direct an electric heater towards your partner. He or she should be naked, hence the need for heat. For if there is only a light draught, he or she may tense. The other vital factors to contribute towards initial relaxation are that you, the masseur, must have warm hands and the massage oil you use must have been warmed. (Warm the oil by floating the oil bottle in warm water.)

Some masseurs like offering the friends a choice of oil. I usually use suntan oil with all the connotations of summer that it brings, but my own masseur uses a choice of Indian perfumed oils with exotic scents such as patchouli, ambergris, jasmine and musk.

A bed may seem the obvious place to carry out your ministrations but, alas, it's rampant with difficulties. A mattress 'gives' too much, your friend becomes slippery and 'bouncy' and you never quite know if he/she or the bed is getting the best deal. So the best thing is the floor with a duvet or sleeping bag on it to alleviate the pressure on the bones.

When you put on the oil, don't pour a little puddle into your hands and then slosh it in the direction of your victim. Even if it is warm – which I emphasise again is vital – the shock of having this dripped or dropped onto apprehensive flesh is considerable.

Rub it into your own hands before you transfer it with quick, matter-of-fact strokes to your partner's back. I am assuming we are starting off by massaging the back because it is the easiest area to get access to without embarrassment.

Cover the entire area to be massaged. This includes the shoulders, the back, any part of the arm exposed, the hands, the waist and the buttocks. You can stop at the top of the legs.

As some of the strokes involve actually kneeling astride your partner, it is both practical and sensual to wear only pants or briefs on your lower half, and a loose, stretchy garment, such as a cotton T-shirt, on your top.

Any time the oil wears off your partner's body, apply more so that there is no roughness or undue pressure on the skin.

Make sure that your hands are clean and that there is no dirt or grit on them. It is sensible to keep your nails trim so that you cannot scratch your partner.

Some of the strokes will naturally feel easier if done at your partner's side, but others, mostly those involving travelling up and down the back, are easier if done from a straddle position, actually sitting on top of your partner's legs.

Do not be afraid of shifting around and making yourself comfortable. Simply keep one hand in touch while you move. And take things easy. It's far more sensual to be massaged slowly than to be rushed at like an old washboard.

THE STROKES

1. *Circles*

The first stroke is to place the palms of both hands on the shoulders and move them in circles, firmly outwards and away from the spine, progressing down the back, along the sides of the body, till you reach the buttocks.

Continue the circling on down the buttocks until you reach the upper parts of the legs where you reverse the process and go back up the body.

When you return to the shoulders, encompass the top part of the arms and end by returning across the shoulders to the neck, where your thumbs should naturally penetrate the hairline and perform a little individual massage of their own.

The circling stroke can be carried out over the back six times and of course the pressure of the stroke can be varied. As you grow more experienced, your fingers will sense the depth that your friend will enjoy. On the last circling session, finish below the buttocks.

2. *The glide*

From the circling stroke you can carry out the next movement, the glide, which I think is the most spectacular part of any massage. Place your hands on the lowest part of your friend's bottom with the palms flat and the fingers pointing towards the head. Then, with the weight of your body directed from the solar plexus, start pushing both hands up along the spine, taking as long as you like.

This is a heavy stroke as you are actually leaning on your friend. And your friend experiences this as a sense of overwhelming ripple, like a wave that flows directly along the back and threatens to break over the head.

When you reach the shoulders and neck, lightly bring your hands down again to the buttocks and recommence. Do this three or four times.

Massage 2: the glide

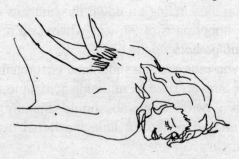

It is important not to break your touch with your partner. If you have to apply extra oil, try to keep part of your body in contact.

3. *Swimming*

This is where the hands, using the palms, move in circles, close together but in opposite directions to each other, taking on a kind of swimming sensation. It can be carried out up and down all the fleshy parts of the body, including the buttocks.

It is a good idea to include the buttocks as often as possible, as this can be the most erotic zone of the back. Touching the bottom can bring on prickles of delicious sensation to the breast, the head and the genitals.

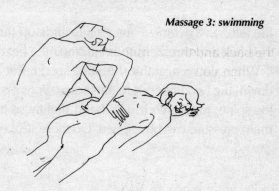

Massage 3: swimming

4. The double-hander

The next stroke is aimed at eliminating the tension that
many people experience in the lower back. Put your right
hand on your friend's buttocks on the right side, with the
fingertips on the waistline, towards the head.

Place the left hand on top of the right one, then circle
towards the hip, the side of the waist and around that
lower back area, leaning your weight on to your hands.
The giant circle that you make around this side of the
bottom can be repeated four times and then carried out on
the opposite side.

5. Thumbing

Working with both thumbs on the lower back, make short,
rapid alternate strokes with each thumb, moving up the
buttocks towards the waist. Carry this on up the right-hand
side of the body to the shoulders, repeat on the left-hand
side, and finish off by concentrating again on the buttocks.

6. Bumps

Sitting by your friend's side, place your right hand on the
base of the spine, fingers pointing towards the head, with

the left hand over it. Then slowly glide up the spine itself. This has a curiously bumpy motion.

Come down again at the same speed. But as you come down, dig two fingers into the indentations on either side of the spine, raising your right hand slightly so that the maximum pressure can be applied. Do these strokes three times.

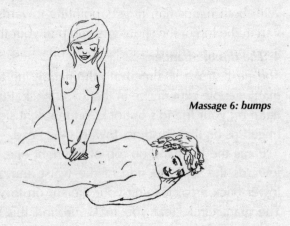

Massage 6: bumps

7. Thumb-pressure strokes

Massage 7: thumb-pressure strokes

By hooking your thumb into the space beneath the shoulder blade, you can create a curious feeling of helplessness. This may be difficult to do if your partner is muscular and the best way to seek out the hollow beneath the shoulder is to lift his or her arm up and fold it across their back. This brings

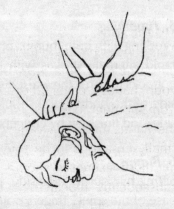

the shoulder blade into sharp relief. Hook your thumb into the hollow side nearest to the spine and slowly rake it through and out towards the armpit. Do this three or four times and then gently place the arm back on the ground. Do the same with the other arm and shoulder blade.

8. *Spinal tap*
With both hands flat, fingers pointing towards the head, start at the top of the shoulders and pull your thumbs, at a deep pressure, down the hollows on either side of the spine, till you reach the buttocks. You can repeat this stroke three times, on each occasion varying the pressure of your stroke.

9. *Thumb glide*
When you reach the buttocks on the third repeat of the spinal tap, make a variation of the glide by putting your full weight behind your thumbs and gliding heavily up your partner's back and finishing in the hairline.

Massage 10: arms

10. *The arms*
Using rapid pulling strokes on one arm at a time with both your hands, cover the area from shoulder to wrist. Once at the hand, there is a variety of small sensations to be sought; all these exercises should be subsequently repeated on the other arm and hand:

a) Hand-to-hand deep palming in circles.
b) With both your thumbs, knead the fleshy parts of your friend's hand. This can be difficult if he or she is thin.
c) Very lightly and slowly, pull your forefingers down between each finger towards the palm, till all four finger spaces have been caressed.
d) Using your fingernails, gently rake the palm and wrist.

The above ten strokes are the basis of a massage. The erotic effect depends on the type of pressures used, the use of your fingernails on the erogenous zones, and the subtlety of where you place your caresses. The strokes described can be varied for the front of the body, the legs, the feet, and even the face.

THE HOMEWORK DAILY SCHEDULE – WEEK TWO
One hour a day.
Continue with the relaxation, breathing and bio-energetic exercises as before. Add the YES/NO exercise, three times a week.

YES/NO exercise

This consists of saying YES to three things you really *want* to do and NO to three things you really *don't* want to do. For example, on one level, if you've been denying yourself chocolate because you believe that you ought to be thinner, but you really fancy a bar, then have one *if you're sure* it's what you want. On another level, one woman in our classes realised how much she wanted to burst out with anger when her lover was thoughtless and caused her pain. Previously she had never dared to express herself because she was afraid it might upset the relationship. But with the YES/NOs she understood that if she came out with her anger as she wanted, she might give each of them a chance to rescue the relationship. Certainly things were getting worse because she was repressing her resentment.

Day 1: Bath and self-massage as before; write your diary, paying attention to your reactions to last night's meeting.

Day 2: Using a small mirror, take some time looking at your genitals. See if you can identify the different parts, such as the clitoris, the urethra and the labia. Think about your feelings. Do you like what you see? Do you like looking? End the session with the breathing exercises as before.

Day 3: Diary day. Record your feelings about your body and your genitals. Think back to yesterday and your thoughts about looking at your genitals. Where do you think your attitudes and reactions to your body have come from? Have they changed as you have grown older?

Day 4: Bath and self-massage as before, spending more time today on the genitals and less on the body.

Day 5: Using your mirror, draw a sketch of your genitals. Remember to bring it to the next group meeting. Genital massage again. Try doing this while watching in the mirror. See how your skin reacts to your touch and don't be afraid of touching the insides of your labia (lips) with clean hands.

Make sure you use a massage oil to make the movement of your hands easier. The inside of your vagina is actually cleaner than the inside of your mouth and it's a good idea to try and become as familiar as possible with how you look, feel and smell. Smell your fingers after you have been touching yourself, taste them too (there is, I repeat, nothing unclean about vaginal secretions). There was one sentence in *The Female Eunuch* by Germaine Greer that stayed with me above all others. 'If you think you are emancipated, you might consider the idea of tasting your menstrual blood – if it makes you sick, you've a long way to go, baby.' Try it and you'll see what Germaine was getting at. Take a note of any changes in your sensitivity to touch. Most women are likely to feel most sensation around the clitoris but you may get reactions around the vaginal opening, at varying levels of the vagina, and, if touched very gently and sensitively, on the cervix.

Day 6: Note down last night's sensations. Make a list of what you might want to talk about to the group. Indulge yourself for the rest of the hour.

Above all, think about the YES/NOs throughout the week. And make sure you don't forget to do them.

ADDITIONAL READING
Erotic Massage by Anne Hooper (Dorling Kindersley, 2005). This is a tastefully illustrated massage manual.

The Little Book of Sex by Anne Hooper (Dorling Kindersley, 2005). It is a small store of sexual information.

Chapter 3

WEEK THREE

Kate dashes in, bursting to tell of her YES/NO decisions. She can hardly wait for the rest of us to assemble before describing her week. As she talks, it becomes very clear that her sex drive is very bound up with her feelings of assertiveness.

TALKING ABOUT THE HOMEWORK

KATE

'I've really thought about my options with Ian.' She's in deadly earnest. 'He's been in touch with me daily, constantly pushing me to live with him again. I don't think he took me seriously when I asked him to move out before. He obviously just thought it was a mood and that it would pass. But I've considered everything carefully and said NO quite firmly to our meandering lives together. It wasn't easy to do, because a lot of me misses him and wants him around, but then a lot more of me can just see how he's been taking advantage of my easy presence. So I'm sticking to my guns.

'But... I also exercised another option. And that was to say YES to our having sex together. I decided that even though I wasn't living with him any longer, I really wanted to make love with him. So we did.

'I'm very pleased that I stuck to my decision because it gave me a new freedom this weekend and some really nice things happened to me. I went to stay with some friends and on the Saturday evening the four of us, two men and two women, were lying around talking. I told them about the massage we did here last week and they all became very interested. I described how free I'd felt after it. I'd thought it was marvellous to enjoy being touched by other women and the whole thing just felt so good. So, suddenly, one of the men said, "Let's try it." And took his clothes off. I felt pretty scared when that happened but excited too. I told myself this is something you want to do, so say YES to it. So I did. I took off my clothes, then the others did too and the four of us began to massage each other.

'I was pretty tense and strung up to start with. But once I was the one being massaged I felt much better. I relaxed and then began to enjoy it. We changed partners, men with men, women with women, and so on, and some of the time we just talked, funny little quips.

'From being a nervous, uptight little bunch, frightened of overexposing ourselves to each other, we expanded our friendship in the nicest ways possible.

'It was surprisingly difficult doing a massage with friends. I suppose everyone is scared of spoiling an already-established pattern of friendship. But afterwards I felt a real sensation of liberation. I'd done something difficult and found out I could enjoy it.'

Shortly after the weekend, Kate had another of her orgasmic dreams. 'I've been having problems with a girl at work who is my assistant. I knew I was going to have a confrontation with her on Tuesday and on Monday night I dreamt about it. In the dream I was saying very forcefully that "there were no two ways about it, I was having my holiday in June and hers would have to be deferred". I remember shouting this out while pounding my fists to emphasise my determination and then I woke up to find myself contracting powerfully in a strong orgasm. It was tremendous. And it happened *twice* that night.

'Next day, at work, there was no problem telling her my holiday arrangements. I didn't have to argue or shout or stamp my feet. I was cool and decisive. I'm getting such a sense of satisfaction to know I can actually *do* things.'

HALEY

Haley too has been practising the massage with her husband. 'I bought a sex magazine on my way home from work,' she tells us. 'It's the first time I've read this one. The train journey home went by unnoticed because I was so absorbed in the readers' letters. What really got through to me was the problems section. I began to realise what pressure we are *all* under to be good at sex. And just finding out I wasn't the only one who was "bad" at sex took a weight off me. I didn't feel so alone.

'When I reached my home station, carrying the magazine under my arm, I went to buy a paper from the newspaper vendor there. "What's that you're reading?" he asked conversationally. So I told him straight out. "Oh yes," he said, "I know that magazine. What do you think of it?" I found myself telling him I'd been having sex problems and that I'd already been feeling better from finding that others were in the same boat. "Oh yes," he looked interested. "I'm in the same situation." And we got into a whole conversation about his problem, which is impotence, and my problem, which I suppose is a female equivalent, and I just thought the whole exchange was fantastic. I can't ever imagine previously having an intimate conversation about my sexuality with a news-paper seller. And I began to realise just how much I could open out. You could definitely say that my being able to talk about sex to this man was a YES.'

Haley's journey home that night had a direct bearing on her massage with Len. 'I think some kind of pressure had been released by all this,' she says. 'Somewhere in my head, I relaxed. That night Len and I decided to do the massage together. I started off by massaging him so that I could show him what I'd learned. And then he did it to me.

'I lay on my stomach and he massaged my back. He straddled me across the thighs and began the glide and circling strokes up and down me. And he got very turned on by it. So did I. I began to make noises of excitement and he became so responsive that he got an erection. After about ten minutes of this, his penis, which had just been hitting me gently every time he bent up to my body, just seemed to find its way into my vagina from that massage position. And very slowly, as he continued massaging me, he also made love to me. I found it unbelievably exciting. Now usually when I reach this stage of excitement, something inside me turns off. But on this occasion I felt open and free.

'And I knew, I just *knew*, I could have an orgasm. We'd never made love in exactly this position before. And I think my clitoris was throbbing against the ground each time he pressed on me. I felt very high up and floating on my excitement. My orgasm was about to take off and fly away any second.

'What actually happened was that I was so near it, it may even have begun very faintly. But I didn't quite get there. The great thing, though, was that it didn't matter. Because Len turned me over and made love to me with his fingers and I came then immediately. But what pleased me so much was I suddenly knew that even if it hadn't quite happened, it could now. I'm sure it can.'

MAGGIE

Maggie, in contrast with Haley, is depressed. This week she hasn't done her homework. 'I live in a flat with a lot of other girls,' she tells us, 'and they're always wandering in and out of the bedroom. I know you're going to say I should lock the door but I think that would be a bit silly. They'd only start banging on it and wanting to know why they're not allowed in.'

It's the new confident Kate who points out the alternative. 'Hang up a notice, saying you want to be very private and that on no account are you to be disturbed until the notice is removed. There's nothing very difficult about that.'

Maggie has to agree. But then she says, 'I'm out all the time. I've got an evening class on one night, go to Pilates for two nights and help a woman friend on another night. There just isn't time. When I come home I'm tired.'

'You sound as though you're making difficulties,' says Mary reflectively. 'I can say that because I can see *this* week how I was *last* week. Don't you want to try and make this course work for you?'

'Yes, of course I do,' says Maggie defensively.

'Then you must do the homework,' I say.

'There doesn't seem much point,' she wails. 'The few times I've tried self-massaging and genital massage nothing happens. I don't feel anything. I don't work. I think I'd rather not start; that way I don't get all keyed up full of expectations.'

'Of course you must start,' says Kate, outraged. 'If you don't start, you'll never find out anything.'

Maggie begins to talk about her mother. 'I know that my mother's solution, in the face of difficulties, is to retreat. If my father gets mad with her, she never retaliates. And she never suggests any alternatives. All suggestions for any family activity come from my father. I've learned from them that nothing I say and do is going to make any difference.'

Shouts from everyone assembled. 'Nonsense!'

'Your YES homework next week,' I say firmly, 'is to make time for yourself, put a notice on the door and persevere with the genital massage. Give yourself a fair opportunity in surroundings where you feel secure, to see what massage and masturbation feel like. It may be that you are somebody who will respond better to a vibrator, but it's sensible to try without one first.'

Maxie hesitantly questions one of Maggie's characteristics. 'Why do you talk in a little-girl voice?' she asks, 'when you feel you are under attack? Is it a way of fending off the grown-ups?'

Maggie is amazed. 'I didn't know I did, ' she eventually manages to say. 'Do you think it matters?'

'Perhaps if you sound more grown-up,' Maxie suggests tentatively, 'people would take more notice of you.'

Maggie says nothing else for the time being but retreats into herself.

MARY

Mary has taken the self-pleasuring part of her homework further than is suggested. 'I enjoyed doing it so much,' she says. 'Bruce was away for a week so I had a lovely clear time to myself. At the beginning I thought the self-pleasuring was going to be a waste of time and I got down to it very reluctantly. But the second night, something really shaped up. I got very hot and very soft, and had loads of different, exciting feelings in my vagina. I decided to see what would happen if I carried on. So I kept moving my fingers around on my clitoris and I came!' She beams around the group, proud of her announcement. We burst into spontaneous 'hoorays', 'congratulations' and clapping. Everyone laughs.

'The next night, needless to say, I was very keen to do my homework. It was a bit harder this time but I could still do it.

'Which is all fine. But the trouble is, when Bruce came home I seemed to clam up. Not immediately, though. The first night I was still sexy after these lovely feelings. For the first time in years I was keen to go to bed with him. Almost to show off, I suppose. And it was all so new, it was exciting for both of us. I decided to see if I could masturbate while he was in me and discovered I could. I came with him inside me which pleased him enormously.'

Mary doesn't look as if it had pleased *her* enormously. 'It doesn't seem to have solved anything between us,' she says wryly. 'I suppose I thought it would. But instead of letting him become more relaxed about sex, it's inspired him to up the pressure. He's on at me all the time to go to bed.

'The other night he did the ironing. I had had a hell of a day with the babies and I was exhausted. And although he too had had a tough day, he did this work for me. Which was marvellous and I appreciated the help. But all the time he was doing it, I was aware of the thought, in the back of his mind, that "maybe, if I do this for her, she'll pay me back by screwing me tonight". It's as if the ironing was a bribe or a barter of some sort.

'And since then I've been unable to come with him. To be quite honest, I've felt so *un*turned on, I haven't even wanted to masturbate.'

Ros was a girl in our first group who'd had a similar relationship. She had tried out the experiment of giving herself and her man certain nights on which they might or might not choose to have sex. Ros had Mondays, Wednesdays and Fridays on which she could say YES or NO to Mark about sex, and Mark had Tuesdays, Thursdays and Saturdays. Sundays were optional.

What happened in practice was that Ros always chose *not* to on her nights and Mark always chose *to* have sex and invariably they did as well on Sundays. Thus the amount of sex was cut by nearly a half.

'It gave each of them responsibility for their own nights,' I explain. 'Ros was no longer pressurised on her nights and Mark began to understand that her decisions were *hers* and not his. They each ended up feeling as if they had choice, instead of only one of them ever having any choice.'

'That does sound like a good idea,' Mary is interested. 'Bruce might agree to that. Maybe I could suggest it to him.'

JAN

'I'm not sure I have much to tell you,' she reports. 'I've thought a great deal about everything said last week about Jim. There are two things which, reluctantly, I've accepted. The first is that I *do* resent him but I realise I haven't let myself admit it before. And the second is that I've reached a stage of disliking him. That's in spite of still finding him attractive. So I find myself in a bind where I want to go to bed with him but then, when I'm there, the angry part of me turns right off him.'

'Could you, on a practical level,' I ask, 'manage without him?'

'Oh yes, of course,' she says. 'I already do in a way. He gives me problems, not help.'

'What about on an emotional level?'

'That's what I've been wondering,' she answers. 'I tried to work out what I'd feel like if he went away. There'd be a lot of relief. But there would also be a scared bit of me that's saying suppose you never get another man.'

Maxie, her friend, chips in. 'I keep telling her she wouldn't find any difficulty in meeting another man. She just keeps saying "but he'll never be as attractive as Jim".'

'It's odd,' says Mary, 'because from the way you've described him he doesn't sound at all attractive. He may be outwardly, but he sounds like an unpleasant person inside.'

Jan looks very worried. 'I know. That's what I'm realising. But I still can't imagine getting turned on by anyone else.'

'Have you tried?' asks Mary. 'Going out with anyone else?'

'I've been out with one or two old boyfriends, but I really didn't enjoy that very much. And I was scared of Jim finding out in case he gets violent. He has hit me on a couple of occasions.'

'Does he hit Will?' asks Maggie.

'No, quite the opposite. When Will was born, he just sat in the hospital and gazed at him. He didn't look at me, didn't speak to me, just drooled over the baby.'

'So he's a good father, is he?' Mary pursues.

'We-ell,' Jan doesn't quite know the answer to that. 'I thought he was going to be. But I've been realising that he has never actually spent any time with Will. Although he thinks Will is marvellous, the extent of his active interest in him is to tell me that I'm continually doing things wrong with the child. Which, since I'm the only one who actively looks after Will, is a bit much. He doesn't like the fact that I work – I do take Will with me – and says this makes me a bad mother, yet he doesn't actually go out and get a job.'

'You really don't need this man,' Haley has been listening open-mouthed, outraged.

'I'm beginning to see that,' agrees Jan despairingly. 'But how do I get him to go without dreadful scenes and how do I cope afterwards when he's gone?'

BREAKING UP

'I don't think you will be able to get him to go without dreadful scenes,' says Mary. 'I lived with a man for five years, before Bruce, who was a little like Jim. He was sometimes violent. And there was no way of busting up with him without terrible scenes. I got to realise after we'd nearly broken up on two occasions that I had to go through the scenes in order to be able to emerge at the other end.'

'Did he hit *you* when you split?' asks Jan.

'Once. There were a couple of other times when I thought he was going to but he didn't. I became quite fatalistic about it. I knew I'd survive but I also grew more and more convinced he would have to go. If he gets really bad, Jan, you could get police protection. I think it would be safest to be prepared for a bad time and act as if it's an emergency even if you turn out not to need this help.'

'How did you feel when your guy went? Afterwards, I mean?' Jan asks.

'Incredible relief. My life was far easier and I didn't give myself time to miss him. I filled my evenings with things to do. I rang up old boyfriends, went to classes, got on to a party circuit. One of the best things was being able to spend more time with girlfriends. I got a lot of support from other women.'

'But I've got a kid. It's not going to be so easy when you've got baby-sitting problems to work out.'

'No, but it's not impossible.' Mary answers.

LIVING ALONE

'It's not the end of the world to live alone,' points out Maggie, who is doing precisely that. 'I thought I'd fall to pieces when my boyfriend went abroad two years ago. But I've liked it. I feel self-sufficient now and I hardly ever get lonely.

'The worst bit is not having anyone to give you an occasional cuddle but I've done so many other things I never had time for previously. And *my* women friends are great too.'

MEETING PEOPLE

'Meeting people seems to be a doddle these days,' I add. 'If it doesn't happen through friends and going to parties, just try the matchmaking websites. I've heard of loads of people meeting their soul mate through those. Yes, you may have to weed through some unsuitables, but I know of four people who have met the man of their dreams and have actually remarried.'

Mary gets jokey. 'You may get flooded with e-mails if you advertise yourself. You could beam them around the group. We might all meet some really gorgeous fellows.'

'That's not such a bad idea,' says Maxie seriously. 'I might join you. If you advertise, I will too. We could sort through them together.'

MAXIE

On that optimistic note, Maxie, always the last, gives her account of last week's homework.

'I'm not sure I really did the YES/NOs in the right way,' she says hesitantly.

'What did you do?' we ask encouragingly.

'Well,' she pauses for a while. 'I decided that I was fed up with my work. I've hated it for a long time but I haven't actually done anything about it. Now I decided I would. So I handed in my notice.'

Gasps from around the room.

'Then,' she continues, 'I realised how much I dislike

living in my present flat and sharing it, so I went out and found another of my own.'

We're quiet now, awestruck, wondering what the next revelation will be.

'And then,' she concludes, 'I realised that the only reason I was going out with my boyfriend was so that I would have someone to go out with and that I didn't even like him. So I gave him up.'

Splutters and gasps from all around.

'Do you think they count as YES/NOs?' The amazing thing is that Maxie is still hesitant.

'I think they count as changing your entire life.' I'm stunned. 'You can't get much more decisive than that.'

The real surprise, of course, is that these momentous personal decisions are coming from the quietest and most unassuming member of the group. After the commotion has died down, Maxie explains that she's taken the risk of becoming a virtual secretary while she makes up her mind what she wants to do full-time.

THE INFO

When the excitement of Maxie's news abates we turn to another aspect of the homework. We take a quick look at the drawings of our genitals, which were part of the week's homework. Next we talk about self-help and knowing your body.

SEXUAL HEALTH

We talk about contraception, abortion, cervical smears, sexually transmitted diseases and the menopause. Each woman contributes her experiences of these and I usually commission one member of the group to make an expedition to the nearest bookshop to bring back several relevant titles. Sometimes, if I feel a book is especially important, I will stock up and hand out copies around the group. Since the aforementioned health subjects are dealt with fully in the books I recommend later (see Additional Reading at the end of this chapter), we will move on here.

SELF-EXAMINATION

The finale of the evening is the self-examination. Using a transparent disposable speculum, I demonstrate, with the aid of a mirror, some lights, a box of tissues and KY jelly (a non-staining, water-soluble jelly available from any chemist), just how to use it and why it's a good idea to do so occasionally.

The unopened speculum is slipped slowly and carefully into the vagina until it reaches as far as it will go. Then I gently click it open. This enables me and the others to see inside my vagina, where the cervix is plainly in view at the end of the vaginal tunnel.

When everybody has looked and has learned how to use the speculum, each woman takes her own from a store I supply (she will keep it hereafter for her personal use) and, in turn, views her cervix, then demonstrates it to us.

Since it is usually the first time that these women have had the opportunity to look at other women's genitals, the task elicits reactions such as 'I'd no idea everyone's genitals looked so different. I'd always imagined they looked the same.' But like faces, genitals are uniquely individual. Betty Dodson's *Sex For One: The Joy of Self-*

Loving illustrates this perfectly with her twelve superbly drawn pictures of different vulvae.

THE VALUE OF SELF-EXAMINATION

What, then, is the value of looking at each other's genitals and cervixes when, in the past, these have been activities reserved mainly for the doctor?

The aim of self-examination is to demystify a part of the body that for hundreds of years has been kept a secret. Originally, of course, no one knew what the inside end of the vagina looked like, but eventually our midwives and doctors found out, and with the advent of modern equipment, such as the speculum, it has become a matter of health routine to examine female patients (as, for example, when you are expecting a baby). Yet a cervical inspection is something that generally takes place when you or the doctor suspects *something is wrong* or, in the case of pregnancy, something has changed. And what that leaves out is an interesting and positive realm of health information that tells you about your body *when you are well*.

By using a speculum regularly you can get to know when your interior looks well or looks inflamed. You can see changes depending on the time of the menstrual month. By looking regularly you can get to know what is normal for you.

We see our faces every morning in the mirror and touch them many times during the day. So we soon become aware of a swelling developing into a spot, or a change in colour and temperature. And yet when this is applied to the genitals many people are shocked.

To some people, a woman who knows her cervix is a woman who might discover information too powerful to handle. She might diagnose herself and not go to the doctor, and an infection might get worse. And anyway, what's the point when she can go to the doctor and he'll look for her and tell her if there's anything she needs to know?

My answer to these attitudes is that a doctor does not see you enough to know what is normal for you. He cannot always be sensitive enough to the subtle changes that would enable him to practise preventative medicine by detecting early signs of infection, disease and pregnancy.

By knowing what is 'right' for us we can remain in control of our sexual health. If self-examination tells us that we ought to see the doctor, then that's useful. If, on the other hand, you can see that everything looks fine, you can rest and relax.

Another value of doing self-examination is to dispel fears we may have about our genitals. Betty Dodson thought for years that hers were deformed because her inner labia (lips) grew when she matured sexually and hung down like 'chicken wattle'. Her relief was great when she found out that hundreds of other women have similarly shaped genitals.

For those who have been brought up to believe that touching yourself down there is 'dirty', it is helpful to understand that the vagina and cervix are as much a clean, functionally useful and common-or-garden part of the body as are the penis and testicles on a man. No man would think himself 'dirty' should he pay hygienic attention to his genitals, and it is thought natural nowadays for little boys to explore themselves. Hopefully, thinking along these lines will make it clearer to women that a natural curiosity about a part of your own body is healthy, and that a knowledge of your genitals is desirable since it is through this that you may keep them clean and well.

GROUP SELF-EXAMINATION

But why do a self-examination in a group? Why not just do it privately, at home? Of course, it is an excellent idea to do it privately. In fact, the best way to get to know the insides of your genitals is to monitor yourself every single day with the speculum over a couple of months, keeping a record of any changes you see in your cervix. This way you get to know what is normal for you at specific times of your monthly cycle.

But the use of doing the self-examination together is that it speeds up the delivery of information about what the inside of the genitals looks like.

- You may see a pregnant woman whose cervix will be a light mauvish colour.
- You may see a woman shortly before her period is due whose cervical colouring will probably be angry-looking and her natural discharge perhaps faintly discoloured.
- Sometimes, in the middle of a woman's menstrual cycle, you may observe drops of blood coming from the cervix, which usually means that she is ovulating.
- You can see that some women possess a shorter vaginal canal than others.
- You can see that the cervix may be located in a variety of positions, and not always in the same place.

Most important of all, group self-examination is the most direct method of finding out that women's genitals are all incredibly different from each other.

At no time should anyone be forced to do a self-examination if she can't face the thought of demonstrating herself publicly. But certainly it can be made clear at both this session and in the previous week that it is a valuable activity to carry out together. When six women trust each other enough to be able to do this, they experience warm friendship as a result.

INSIDE THE VAGINA

The non-pregnant uterus is about the size and shape of a pear. The big back end of the pear stretches up into the abdomen, but the small, narrow end (cervix) comes down into the vagina. When the speculum is used, it holds apart the vaginal walls and exposes the cervix and the os.

The os is the entrance to the narrow cervical canal that leads to the uterus. Women who have not had a child have a small, round os. Women who have had a child have a slit-shaped one.

Nancy MacKeith is the author of the first handbook to discuss the subject of self-examination, *The New Women's Health Handbook* (see Additional Reading at the end of this chapter). She also runs self-help groups, and explains, 'Women who don't know themselves have concepts of huge caverns inside them. Sometimes they fear they can lose a tampon inside their uterus. If you've ever had that kind of fear, it's a fantastic relief to realise that it could never happen.'

HEALTH ISSUES TO LOOK OUT FOR DURING SELF-EXAMINATION

The following section is based on an article from *Forum* magazine written by Nancy MacKeith, which is as relevant now as it was when it first appeared in 1976.

MENSTRUATION

It is as safe to use a speculum during menstruation as it is to have sex. But women still need reassurance about this. In many women the os widens slightly during a period, presumably to let the blood out. This is why women are advised that the best time to have an IUD (coil) fitted is when they are menstruating because then they don't have to be dilated so much.

By examining yourself regularly you can follow the menstrual cycle and discover the days of your ovulation. This enables a woman to use an updated natural rhythm method of birth control or to conceive if she wants to.

MENSTRUAL CYCLES

Since the Pill, more and more women have the idea that they are abnormal if they don't have a 28-day cycle. This is the result of the false 28-day cycle induced by oral contraception. We can show women that they are still ovulating on a three-week cycle or a six-week cycle. We do this by daily observation of the cervix. After menstruation the cervix is very clear with little secretion. Nearing ovulation we see a variety of secretions from the os. We can recognise the time of ovulation from the changes in the secretions.

PREGNANCY

The cervix of many pregnant women becomes a veiny blue. Other visual signs are pigmentation around the anus, a line showing between the pubic hair and the navel, a change in the colour of the cervix from pale pink to darker pink, and increased secretion.

'It's possible to diagnose pregnancy within a week of conception, provided you know what your interior looks like normally.' Nancy confirmed that she diagnosed her own pregnancy within one week. 'This is very valuable because you know immediately that you should stop taking drugs, drinking, should eat well and should give up smoking.'

Nancy continued to view her cervix during pregnancy. 'As time advanced, the colour became darker and darker, and the secretions increased.'

DISCHARGES AND SECRETIONS

There are several varieties of vaginal secretion, which can be separately identified. A substance looking like egg white, which appears at ovulation time or pre-period time, is identified as a secretion. If it smells bad or if there is suddenly much more than usual, or if it is blood-streaked, it is called a discharge.

White discharge lining the cervix is identified as 'thrush'. Thrush may be due to a slight metabolic imbalance, or to being diabetic, being on the Pill, being on antibiotics or eating too much sugar. Thrush may be cured by coming off the Pill, or ceasing to take antibiotics (but speak to your doctor first), or with Canestan or any recommended anti-thrush medication. The old-fashioned method of curing thrush is to insert live natural yogurt into the vagina. The yogurt changes the environment of the vagina, making it unfavourable to yeast spores, which cause the itch.

Self-treatment isn't always appreciated by the medical profession. 'We could treat ourselves far more than we do,' Nancy explains. 'But we meet with some strong objections from doctors if we do. An example of this is with trichomoniasis. Doctors use Flagyl (metronidazole) for treating it. This is yellow, bubbly and smells awful. It is also a very strong drug. We have discovered that garlic can cure "trich" but I know that if I start recommending this, doctors will be outraged.'

CERVICAL SMEARS

If, viewed through the speculum, a red patch is seen, it may be a cervical erosion. Women seeing this should seek a cervical smear, in case of cancer of the cervix. Although it must be emphasised that an erosion is not necessarily an indication of pre-cancerous cells, a smear is a safeguard. In any case, every woman should have regular smear tests, once a year.

There may be a variety of reasons for cervical erosion. The woman may not be looking after herself by eating the right things. A change in diet can often clear up the condition. Eating more vegetables and meat usually helps. So can a local application of warm honey.

IUD (COIL)

The use of a speculum enables a woman to locate her IUD by making it possible for her to see the string dangling from the cervix. It is recommended that IUD users check constantly that the string is in place, as a guide to the safety of this contraceptive device.

Self-help groups have found that the cervixes of many women with IUDs look unhealthy. Typical symptoms may be a small red patch and a discharge coating the string.

There is no proven theory on how the IUD works, but it certainly irritates and disturbs the inside of the uterus, hence the extra discharge.

'I sometimes hear from newly pregnant women who were IUD users,' says Nancy, 'that they had antibiotics around the time they conceived. It is possible that these drugs would cancel out the effect of the IUD, thereby removing the obstacle to conception.'

With this possibility in mind, self-help groups recommend that IUD users should take additional birth-control precautions when using antibiotics.

THE MYTH OF THE RETROVERTED UTERUS

Nancy MacKeith projects a collection of coloured slides at her self-help talks to demonstrate interior anatomical differences. One of her slides shows a woman with the angle of her cervix tilted and the os looking up. This is what doctors term a 'retroverted uterus'. Nancy objects to the description since it sounds as though it is abnormal.

'The only thing that could be called abnormal is the position of the os. The more usual position is at the end of the vaginal canal looking straight at you. It is variously described as twisted or bent. I've even known women who have been told that their retroverted uterus might make them sterile. In actuality, there's no problem about becoming pregnant because sperm can go round that slight bend quite easily.'

EXTRA SKIN

Women often worry about extra skin – small flaps of skin outside or inside the entrance to the vagina. They may worry about one labium being smaller than the other. Self-help groups have found that most women have an extra piece of skin somewhere. *It's normal*. We also recognise that most people have discrepancies in the size of their vaginal lips.

Says Nancy, 'I've given talks where women have practically fought to get down on the mattress first and have a look at themselves with the speculum. We use the transparent plastic sort and with the aid of lights and a mirror it's perfectly possible for every woman to see the inside of her own vagina and her own cervix. They can't wait to look at this mysterious place where traditionally only doctors have been allowed to go.

'They like to find out that a pelvic examination need not be painful. They feel reassured when, after childbirth, they find that their interiors look surprisingly normal. Being able to view their own clitoris and urethra is reassuring.'

Women (and men) are afraid of the great unknown. The interior female genitals have for hundreds of years been a place of mystery. Women have had strange and sometimes frightening concepts of what is inside them. Now they can see for themselves; it's a step on the road to self-knowledge.

Self-knowledge does away with fear and superstition and enables women to have self-respect. When you possess self-knowledge, you possess potential control over your body.

HOW TO USE A SPECULUM

Before attempting insertion, assemble everything you may need for the procedure, such as mirrors, tissues, KY jelly and a light. The speculum should be lubricated with water-soluble jelly (KY). The best position in which to attempt insertion is half-sitting, half-lying, propped against cushions, a mattress or even a wall.

The blades of the speculum are held together to avoid pinching the wall of the vagina, and insertion takes place with the handle held upwards. If the insertion feels shaky, just do it very slowly – there is no hurry. After penetration is complete, the handle can be squeezed gently so that the ratchet opens the blades.

The speculum can be opened one notch at a time until the cervix is visible. In the textbook the cervix lies directly at the back of the vaginal opening. In actual fact it can be located at a variety of angles, and you may have to move the speculum around cautiously until the cervix and os come into view. When you have finished looking, the speculum can be removed by pulling slowly and firmly. It is *not* necessary to close it first.

It is not easy to juggle with the mirror, speculum and light all at the same time. It is therefore sensible, until you grow accustomed to using the speculum, to practise with a friend.

Specula can be obtained from surgical suppliers in most major cities. The Yellow Pages telephone directory usually lists these or you can try looking online.

THE HOMEWORK DAILY SCHEDULE – WEEK THREE
One hour a day.
Repeat the breathing, bio-energetics and YES/NO exercises as before. Add the Kegel exercises.

HOW TO DO THE KEGELS
Kegels are routine exercises often recommended to women after they have had babies, which are aimed at improving the muscle tone of the vagina. Named after their inventor, Dr Kegel, many women have found that after about six weeks of practising, they experience increased pleasure during sexual intercourse. Exercising these muscles increases sensitivity in the vaginal area and also helps to reduce spontaneous urination with orgasm.

To find your PC (pubococcygeal) muscle, practise stopping the flow of your urine next time you go to the lavatory. The muscle that you use to slow down and stop the flow is the PC muscle. Practise stopping the flow several times in order to get used to it. Then lie down, and placing your finger into your vagina, squeeze the PC muscle again. See if you can feel the contractions on your finger.

Exercise No. 1
This consists of squeezing the PC muscle for three seconds then relaxing it for three seconds, then repeating this. Do this ten times, on three separate occasions, every day. The beauty of the Kegels is that no one needs to know you are doing them. You can do them while standing at the bus stop or doing the gardening or the washing-up. The muscles surrounding your anus may also move at the same time, but if you find you are moving your stomach muscles, thigh muscles or buttocks then you are squeezing the wrong muscles.

Exercise No. 2
Do the first exercise, only faster, so that your vagina 'flutters'. It's a bit like a tongue twister in that you can't always be sure you are doing it right. But as your muscles become stronger with practice, you should be able to 'flutter' more easily. Do this ten times, three times a day.

Exercise No. 3

Pretend that the inside of your vagina is a lift (elevator). Your job is to move that lift up your vagina, stopping at three stops on the way. When you reach the fourth and highest stop, hold the lift there for a while, before carefully descending again, pausing at each stop before reaching ground floor again. Try this twice a day.

Constant routine practice of the Kegels strengthens the vaginal muscle so that, because your vagina is stronger, hopefully your orgasm will be too.

Day 1: Bath and self-massage. Genital massage as before, noting any sensations, however small, any changes in feelings, sensitivity to touch, pressure and rhythm.

Day 2: Continue with genital exploration, taking plenty of time; don't aim at having an orgasm, just pay attention to the feelings that you are experiencing, however small. The aim is to build on these, to slowly remake connections that have been disconnected and disused for ages.

Day 3: Examine your cervix with a speculum again.

Day 4: Read *Sex For One* by Betty Dodson (see Additional Reading, below).

Day 5: Bath and self-massage. Continue with self-exploration.

Day 6: Indulge yourself. Try and do the most sensual thing you can think of that you might enjoy. Prepare ideas for the group.

Throughout this week and indeed every week, make use of your diary. Record in it all your self-discoveries, your feelings and your experience of the group. Once again pay attention to the YES/NOs and think how to apply them to your everyday life.

ADDITIONAL READING

Our Bodies, Ourselves, edited by the Boston Women's Health Book Collective (Touchstone Press, 2005). Absolutely everything you need to know about your body and its health.

The New Woman's Health Handbook, edited by Nancy MacKeith (Virago, 1978). A few copies are available from Amazon. The first book of its kind, it describes sexual self-examination and how to understand your natural body changes.

Sex For One: The Joy of Self-Loving by Betty Dodson (Random House, 1996). This ground-breaking book is famous mainly for its striking pencil drawings of women's vulvae, making it crystal clear just how different one woman is from another.

Chapter 4

WEEK FOUR

Week Four does not include any bodywork and often feels disappointing. But since everyday life does not consist of a continual barrage of astounding and stimulating self-revelation, it's not a bad idea to bring the group back to more mundane reality. One of the saddest things I heard from a past member – who had been lifted entirely out of a bad depression by the group – was that her life became an anti-climax once the course finished and she developed, for a while, an even greater depression than before. She did eventually overcome it, but it brought home to me the necessity of planting participants' feet firmly on the ground prior to Week Six.

In addition, people who have religiously been practising the self-pleasuring homework and yet are getting very little genital sensation out of it (they always report good overall body feelings) begin to despair by this stage unless some practical alternatives are suggested.

Therefore, today I introduce the vibrator. I do not believe it's a good idea to struggle on with only the muted sensations that some women experience during genital massage, since they lose heart. But neither do I believe that learning to touch and caress our genitals by hand is a step that should be left out. It's a vital step towards feeling comfortable with our bodies and with sex.

INTRODUCING VIBRATORS

I arrive at the meeting equipped with an assortment of vibrators and pass them around the room. There is the plain, basic, cigar-shaped battery vibrator, which is the cheapest to buy. There are now dozens of gorgeous variations of the plain vibrator easily available from women-only sex shops and from reputable Internet websites (see the list at the end of this chapter). They come in glowing jelly colours and in a variety of sizes and speeds. It's still possible to buy the massive mains-operated models such as the Magic Wand by Hitachi. There are funny little ball-shaped vibrators, which have only a very mild vibration, and there are some very interesting, fit-in-the-hand shaped models, specially designed to thrum on the clitoris. The most famous vibrator at the moment is the Rabbit, notoriously used by Samantha in *Sex and the City* and in major demand ever since.

VIBRATOR MERITS

- The massive *mains-operated* versions are probably the most powerful in terms of speed of vibration but are big, heavy and intrusive. It's hard to keep one discreetly by the side of the bed. However, speed of vibration can sometimes be crucial.
- The *ball-shaped* vibrators are no more than toys. They would not help anyone with serious difficulties in climaxing because they are not powerful enough.
- The *traditional cigar-shaped* models are the most useful for pre-orgasmic women because they are

discreet, powerful enough and can be incorporated in lovemaking with a partner at a later stage, if desired.

- The *Rabbits* (various makes and models) are duel in that they have one small projection that works on the clitoris while a larger one moves differently and separately inside the vagina. Some models even have an extra finger that projects into the anus for additional sensation. The sensation this multiple-movement machine offers is fantastic but probably not if you are only just learning to climax. For someone who is struggling with the concept of using a vibrator in the first place, the Rabbit would be overload. In addition, it's designed very much for women only and it really wouldn't help any problems that may be considered as joint by male and female partners. So although I rave about its merits, the Rabbit goes on the back burner for a more advanced stage of sexual awakening.

- Finally, there is the good old electric toothbrush. Yes, toothbrush – but, I hasten to add, the brush part, the bristles, are naturally all removed by you before you begin to use it at the opposite end of the body for which it was originally designed...

I emphasise the desirability of using long-life batteries with the non-mains models since they last much longer and are much more powerful. Very often when a battery vibrator seems ineffective it's simply because the battery needs renewing. And they wear out surprisingly quickly, which can be an unhelpful let-down.

I suggest the group uses the vibrators in their homework much as they've been using their fingers in the past week. We don't dwell much on the subject but promise to discuss our experiences next week when we've had a chance to experiment.

TALKING ABOUT THE HOMEWORK

MAXIE

Maxie reports some sexy sensations while practising the Kegel exercises. 'My vagina feels wide open and yearning. If I touch or stroke my genitals after doing the Kegels for a while they feel very sensitive. At one stage when I was lying on my back doing them, I arched my back to lift my genitals up higher and my vagina gave a kind of gasp as though it were expelling air. Now, every time I try, I can make this gasp. It's like a contraction.'

Vaginal Gasp

Not every woman is able to make a vaginal 'gasp' at will. It tends to be for those women whose body movements and muscles are well co-ordinated. But practising the Kegels is a good method of toning up the vaginal muscles and can help to build up sexual tension by getting your vagina to 'gasp' at will. It can be used consciously during peaks of sexual excitement to intensify your experience. Some women, capable of multiple orgasms, purposely arch their pelvis after the initial climax while continuing with

either self-stimulation or intercourse. They find that
this sometimes triggers off another – or even several
– climaxes.

Maxie is feeling pleased. Her boss has told her how sorry
she is that Maxie is leaving her job. 'But it's come too late,'
says Maxie. 'It's such a pity she couldn't have made me feel
useful or wanted before. It's taught me how good it is to be
openly appreciative of people. But if I hadn't been so firm
about leaving I'd never have wrung that admission out of
her. So in future I'm going to let my contacts know how
much I value them. It's also taught me that people do react
forcefully and positively to strong self-confidence. I've been
pretty ineffectual in the past, especially with boyfriends. I
know I'm going to be better off on my own at the moment
than with a man I dislike. My resolution to give up Don
hasn't wavered a bit. I feel I'm becoming a whole person.'

JAN

'What's happened to your boyfriend?' Kate asks Jan.

'He's still around,' she tells us. 'We've been having
rows all week. The other night, when we made love, I did
try to bring myself off while he was inside me. I've not tried
this before but I can see it could be a help. Jim, however,
was very impatient with me. It upset him, he said, put him
off his stroke. So in the end I just gave up and lay there.
And that ended by making him angry. Finally he got up,
put his clothes on and stamped out, saying he was going
to find another woman who would behave more naturally
with him, "more like a real woman" were his exact words.'

'Did he go to another woman?' we ask.

'Yes, because the next night we had a tearing row with

me in tears all over him. I couldn't do anything properly, he kept saying, including making love. I wasn't a normal woman. And then of course he started telling me about a woman who did respond "normally". And it only took a bit more screaming at each other for him to come out with the fact that he went to bed with this woman last night, that she welcomed him with open arms and that they had simultaneous orgasms – he kind of flung that in my face.

'I've been desperately hanging on to my own belief that I'm OK. *I* know I can function OK as a woman. It's been getting clearer and clearer to me why I don't relax with him. The more I think about him, the more I can see why I've been living in a continual state of tension ever since I've known him.

'Thinking about the way I climax when I masturbate I can see the pattern of how I get turned on. I can come in about five minutes or even less if I want to. But it takes certain types of movement on my clitoris to get me going. I have tried tactfully with him, often, to get him to do some of these things to me. I have tried in the past showing him or doing it while he was fucking me. I think he's frightened. I think he's terrified that this is a way of me saying *he's* ineffectual. So he gets in first with the accusations. It's hopeless getting good sex together with him. He blocks it off; he won't talk. So what can I do? There doesn't seem much point in going on.'

'What about being so attracted to him, though?' asks Mary. 'Aren't you still feeling that?'

'Ye-es,' says Jan. 'But it's finally got through to me there's not much point. Nothing is going to work with him. He's not letting it. So, somewhere along the line I think I've switched off him. It happened when he stayed out that night.

'I still feel pretty hopeless about being able to fancy some other men, but I've agreed to keep Maxie company with some Internet dating. It's the least I can do to get myself feeling independent again.

'And Will's another matter. All this screaming and rowing is going on in front of him. And I know it's wrong, that it's hurting him. Jim actually picked him up and started thrusting him at me, saying I didn't care about him. And it's not true. I've been slogging myself stupid because I care for the kid so much. It's because of Will I've been so reluctant to admit Jim isn't going to work out. And he's started using the child as a weapon which is a terrible thing to do.' And Jan burst into angry tears.

Immediately, murmurs of comfort and concern come from us all. Maxie puts her arms around her and the rest of us back Jan, saying *we* think she's effective and caring, and that she's an attractive and sexy woman.

KATE

Kate, particularly, is in great sympathy with Jan. She has been psychologically wrestling with her boyfriend too, only in a rather different way.

'He still doesn't believe what I say,' she tells us. 'He's still trying to manoeuvre me into letting him come back to live with me. I know I'm doing the right thing by being firm with him but it's hard. He's using real emotional blackmail now. But if I let him come back we'll just sink into that unsatisfactory state where he treats me like a full-time wife while he opts to be a part-time husband. It may be OK for *him* but it isn't what I want.'

This week Kate looks tired and white. There are black

rings under her eyes. 'He's saying now that he's beginning to realise he does value me. He's even throwing the word marriage into the conversation. And it's making it all so difficult. I would like to get married. And if I were sure Ian meant all the same things about marriage that I do, I'd love to marry him. I can't tell you how much I want to believe him. But I'm not at all sure I do.'

'What do you want from marriage?' asks Haley.

'Well, children of course,' replies Kate. 'But there's got to be an equal partnership between us. I'm happy to allow Ian a lot of freedom in his life provided I have the same freedom. What I just won't contemplate any longer is a double standard. And since that's what we've always had in the past, there's got to be a lot of rethinking on his part before we're going to reach my idea of a good marriage.'

She goes on to talk about using the speculum. 'I found it very hard to bring myself to put it inside me,' she says. 'In fact, I'm still finding it very hard to feel OK about my genitals. I didn't like looking at them in the mirror much. I was certainly very interested to see you demonstrate the speculum last week but I was scared to use it myself.'

How does she feel about touching during the self-pleasuring homework? 'I can touch myself on the outside. I've got used to that. In fact, I like it. It's feeling good, but not, I'm sad to say, orgasmic. But I still don't like putting my finger inside. It seems all wrong.'

How does she feel about her boyfriend penetrating her during intercourse? 'That's fine. If it's someone doing it to me that seems right. But if it's me, it seems wrong and dirty. I know it's ridiculous. I think I must have been slipped some powerful anti-genital conditioning somewhere along the line as a child. Maybe it stems from that time Dad saw me touching myself there.'

MARY

Mary is nodding her head with fellow-feeling. Mary is the one who said that touching your genitals was a 'lesbian' thing to do. But Mary is also the one who learned to masturbate to orgasm ahead of anyone else in the group.

'It was the massage,' she says, 'that changed my ideas about being touched. I was pretty appalled when I realised I was going to have to take my clothes off and be touched by other women. But I told myself, "Now that you're here you might as well try it," and I forced myself to lie down. Then once the massage began it was so good that I didn't care who was touching me just as long as it went on. You could have massaged me all night and I wouldn't have minded. I don't know if anyone else felt like this, but I got very turned on. I simply hadn't realised how marvellous it is to be touched. And I reached a stage where if the person massaging me had included the genitals, I not only wouldn't have minded it, I'd have adored it. And that was in spite of it being a woman who was doing the massage.

'And afterwards I felt so good and caring about all of you. We'd had this very intimate experience together and I hadn't minded. So it seems as if my feelings about women must have changed. I can't see myself ever getting into a lesbian relationship but if other women want to, I can accept how it might happen and I don't feel it's wrong any more.

'After the massage I went home and practised the self-pleasuring properly for the first time. It finally made sense. I know I included the genitals rather earlier than you'd instructed but they felt left out otherwise.

'I find it extraordinary that I could have changed my attitudes so quickly, but I have. I'm beginning to understand how ignorant I've been about my body. I haven't known anything about it. It amazes me it's taken all these years to discover it.'

Mary carries on to talk about Bruce. She repeats what she said last week, which is that she finds it impossible to get aroused by him.

'We have been trying out the contract you suggested last week. He thought that was a good idea. So far we've made love every night it's his night and never on my nights. Which is OK. At least it means I'm getting some kind of breathing space. And he has stopped constantly nagging me about sex, which is a relief. But try as I will, I can't seem to fancy him.'

'Do you fancy anyone else?' asks Maxie.

'Well, yes,' admits Mary. 'I'm constantly meeting men who turn me on. There are actually two fellas around who I'm having sort of affairs with. One is an old boyfriend who's been around on and off for nearly four years. I go to bed with him occasionally. Bruce knows about him, even though he doesn't know I'm still going to bed with him. But I never climaxed with John either, and I'm not sure I could. But there's a new man I met about two months ago whom I've seen a couple of times.'

'How do you feel about him?' asks Kate. 'Do you fancy him?'

'Yes, I do,' she replies. 'A lot. And now I can masturbate I'm pretty certain that if get a chance to go to bed with him I could climax with him.'

'So where does Bruce fit in to all this?' I ask.

'When I first knew Bruce,' she replies, 'I fancied him very much. But then I'd fancied the man I'd lived with previously a lot at the beginning of that relationship too. What I've been reluctantly realising is that there's a mechanism in me that, once I've become familiar with someone, slowly turns me off them.

'I can see that if, hypothetically, I moved in with this new man, Caz, the same thing would happen eventually with him too. So there's no point in changing my man again. Anyway, I value Bruce as a husband. He's a marvellous man in most respects. I like the life I lead with him. I love our family. I know a lot of my problems revolve at the moment around the fact that I'm dog-tired from coping with two very young children. And he's immensely supportive with them. He does everything he can to help me. So it isn't that I'm itching to leave him. I'm not, quite the opposite. But what I have got to do is work out what to do with my sex urge as well as stay married. I know I've made strides by learning to masturbate.'

OPEN MARRIAGE

'Are you talking about opening up your marriage?' asks Haley.

'Well, agreeing to be more open and honest with each other in our marriage, agreeing to give each other space, time off, allowing each other friends who may or may not be sexual friends.

'In a way we do that already,' Mary frowns in con-
centration. 'I know about the occasional times he's had an
affair with someone else and he knows, to some extent, about
my old boyfriend.'

'You can both cope with that, can you?' I ask. 'Aren't
you jealous of each other?'

'I was very jealous of him originally but since I've had
the children he's made it plain how much he loves me. I'm
more secure now. I don't think our marriage is going to
bust up.'

'Is he jealous of you?' I pursue.

'I think he was until he had an affair himself. He saw
that I wasn't going to leave him when I knew about it. And
that made him a lot less insecure about me. You see, I do
need him a lot. He gives me great security. And he knows
that. So he doesn't feel insecure any more either. Which
means that we've stopped being jealous. It's only the sex
thing that's the problem.'

'What's it like when you make love?' asks Jo, my assistant.

'It's not spontaneous,' Mary winkles up her nose. 'It's
mechanical. I don't lie there like a lump, though. I move
around a lot and I'm sexy for him. I like being sexy for him.
It's just that even though we know now how to make me
come, it's still too mechanical to get me excited.

'He gave me two orgasms last week which were very
nice but they've come a bit too late. I felt like a robot. I'm
conditioned to *not* being turned on by him. When I look
at him, I don't see a man who excites me. I see the man
who's spent all those years badgering me for sex!'

'It's only been a week of your new arrangement, for
heaven's sake,' I say. 'You're not giving either of you a

chance to readjust. You can't expect a relationship to change overnight. It may take you as long as another year or more to find the sexual balance. But at least you've begun. It sounds to me as though you've got a very good relationship, which has needed for some time to be enriched by your getting something sexual out of it. You've made a great start.'

'You're probably right,' Mary acquiesces. 'It *is* early days.'

MAGGIE

Maggie too reports getting good tingling sensations in the genitals. She *did* hang a sign outside her door and her flatmates have respected her need for privacy.

'I've been talking to one of the women I share with,' Maggie tells us. 'She was very interested in the self-examination. We did one together on me while she held the mirror and the light. I'd like another speculum so that she can try too. We're going to monitor ourselves every day and keep a record of our body changes.'

This is the first time Maggie has spoken to anyone outside the group about her personal life. It is also the first friendly overture she has made to anyone. One of the facts that emerged when she first talked to the group was that although she is always very busy with her social activities, she didn't have any close friends.

Maggie has done her YES/NOs this week. She has arranged to go on a further course to learn more about assertion and how to gain self-confidence. She's asked her mother to stay with her in town, and not her father. 'It will give her a break. I feel guilty about not asking my father too but he wouldn't fit into my flat and he'd dampen me down so effectively that I and my mother would lose out any chance to be ourselves and to be comfortable. So I decided to say NO to inviting him. I also determined to do the homework every single night this week and I managed it. That's my YES. I feel very pleased about carrying that resolution through.

'I got some happy feelings from the homework. In fact,' her voice goes quieter and childlike again, 'I might actually have had an orgasm but I'm not quite sure. I did get spontaneous waves of feeling but then they seemed to wither away and die.'

'Maybe you're on the brink but can't quite let yourself go,' I suggest. 'Perhaps part of you panics when you get near to climax and switches you off. Next time you reach this point, *make* yourself go on with the stimulation and try to "open" your genitals to it. Think some sexy thoughts to help carry you into orgasm.' (Next week we will talk about using fantasy to aid orgasm.)

HALEY

Haley is low this week since she and Len have not been able to repeat last week's near-orgasm during intercourse. But she has stopped faking and is talking openly to Len about their sex life together.

'He's bringing me off every time with his fingers,' she says. 'We're going through a really good time together. But I still haven't made it during intercourse.'

'Why is that so important?'

She stops to think. 'It's not as important as it used to be,' she says eventually. 'I feel better for being able to come at all with Len. Much better…

'Another thing we've been doing is my masturbating myself while he kisses and cuddles me. I can come like that too. Which is lovely. I can see that I'm lucky to be able to do these things at all. It's just that I would like occasionally for us to both come at the same time while we're fucking.'

THE INFO

The second half of this week's meeting is devoted to a description of what happens physically to a woman's body when she has climaxes. It's based on solid sexological research but is interpolated with observations and gleanings from other women. In case you think this sounds like Biology Class No. 101, it may interest (and bother) you to know that most women find something they *didn't* know about their own anatomy in the following descriptions.

THE PHYSIOLOGY OF ORGASM
An orgasm has been described as a body reflex, akin to a sneeze. It actually is a physiological reflex, which occurs as a response to sensual stimulation. It may be an all-over body response, it may be experienced solely around the clitoris, the sensations may suffuse the entire pelvic area, and the orgasmic contractions may be experienced in the vagina, anus and uterus.

One of the most ignored features of climax is that as the body's responses begin, your brain temporarily loses conscious control and clocks you out to some kind of timeless state. But the main part of orgasm consists of rhythmic contractions emanating from the clitoris.

Of course, how and where the orgasm is experienced is purely individual. Some women talk of overlapping excitement in their breasts or even their ears, which they describe as mini-orgasm. Sex researchers would probably dismiss this description since they would argue the sensations were those of extreme excitement, which can sometimes be confusing. But since these experiences are subjective, who's to say that they are not orgasms?

SEXUAL RESPONSE CYCLE

There are two main explanations of the sexual response cycle, which, to a great extent, blend from one to the other. The first is that proffered by the famous US sex researchers William H Masters and Virginia E. Johnson and was literally the first to be based on solid laboratory research. The second builds on Masters and Johnson's 'discoveries' and takes them further – these are the theories of Chicago-based psychologist and sex therapist Helen Singer Kaplan, based on her clinical observations from over twenty years.

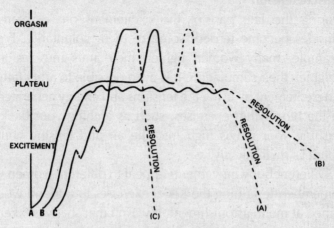

The female sexual response cycle

MASTERS AND JOHNSON'S THEORIES

This pioneering couple saw the sexual response cycle as very similar for men and for women. According to their classification system, the cycle has four phases: the excitement phase, the plateau phase, the orgasmic phase and the resolution.

FEMALE RESPONSE

Excitement

The first sign of the *excitement phase* is vaginal lubrication. The vagina lengthens and distends, and the vaginal walls change to a darker hue due to engorgement with blood. This blood engorgement, which in men is responsible for filling and elevating the penis, in women fills and elevates the labia and the clitoris. She literally has an erection, only in her case it's of all areas of her genitals.

Muscle tension

During the late part of the excitement phase, many muscles become tensed, some of them voluntarily. For example, many women tighten their anus muscles to heighten their stimulation. It is even possible to artificially aid excitement by using the tensions and energy generated in the bio-rhythm exercises, such as arching your back, pushing your pelvis high into the air and tensing your buttocks rhythmically.

Different body movements appeal to different women. I remember describing the Kegel exercises to a friend who gaped at me in astonishment. It wasn't that she was taken aback by the thought of exercising the sexual part of her body; rather, that for years she had been regularly contracting her vagina as I'd described *in order to reach her orgasm*.

Recently I practised some bio-energetic exercises with a woman who confessed to being very scared of letting her body-energy flow in order to achieve the kind of body vibration we aim at. 'My body vibrates anyway when I masturbate,' she said. 'It's how I come. But I'm so ashamed of it. I try to stop it when I make love with my present boyfriend.' Perhaps not surprisingly she was unable to climax with him. When she described herself during sexual excitement, it appeared that her entire body shook like a leaf to the point that her free hand danced around her hips involuntarily.

Another woman at the same bio-energetic class told us that she lifted her hips right off the ground during masturbation almost as if she were limbo dancing in order to gain pelvic tension.

At this stage of excitement the nipples usually become erect, and with women who have not breastfed, the entire breast will fill out as sexual tension increases. There is no noticeable difference, however, in the breast size of women who have suckled.

At the height of the excitement phases, 75 per cent of women develop a 'sex flush'. This is a measles-like rash that spreads rapidly from under the rib cage and all over the breasts.

Plateau phase
In the second phase of orgasm, the *plateau phase*, the outer third of the vagina closes a little due to the swelling

caused by the increased blood supply. Masters and Johnson have called this distended part of the vaginal wall the 'orgasmic platform'. The engorged inner lips at this stage undergo a striking colour change, though of course most of us are not in a position to observe it. In women who have never given birth they change from pink to bright red, and in women who have given birth from red to a deep wine colour.

The tricky bit about the plateau phase is that during this level of increased sexual tension, the clitoris, that key factor in all this excitement, seems to disappear. In fact it is simply hidden in the folds of engorged flesh, which rise around it. This doesn't usually matter if it's you who is doing the stimulating because you can still retain a fair idea of where the good feelings are, but if it's your partner making with the fingerwork, he or she has a tough time since he/she is no longer certain if he/she is stimulating the right part. A little 'left hand down' here is a distinct help.

The tissues around the nipples swell with fluid so that the nipple erection also seems to disappear while the sex flush spreads to some or all parts of the body.

Orgasm

At the moment of *orgasm* (phase three), breathing is at least three times as fast as it would be normally. An additional way of artificially building up excitement is by consciously speeding up breathing and making it shallower. Further, the heartbeat is more than double its usual rate and blood pressure is increased by one-third. Most of the body muscles are tense (see Week One homework).

No one has yet worked out exactly what it is that triggers the orgasmic response but climax begins with contractions starting in the orgasmic platform in the outer third of the vagina. This platform contracts rhythmically as sexual tension is released. The contractions begin at 0.8 second intervals and recur from three to fifteen times, decreasing in frequency and intensity after the first few. Sometimes the uterus contracts simultaneously, sometimes the anus. Pregnant women often experience these contractions in the stretched uterus and can actually feel them ripple across their belly.

Physiologically, orgasm is a release of the muscular tension and engorgement of blood vessels built up during sexual excitement. Subjectively, climax is a peak of physical pleasure. Aesthetically, it is what birth-control pioneer Marie Stopes described as bliss!

Resolution phase
After the orgasms comes phase four, the *resolution phase*, when the body returns to its unstimulated state. All the physiological signs of tension and blood engorgement dissipate during the process of 'returning to normal'.

MULTIPLE ORGASMS
Where women differ from men in their sexual response cycle is that after they have reached orgasm, some of them, instead of rapidly going through the resolution phase, simply drop back into the plateau phase again, whence they can reach, either once or several further times, more climaxes. However, please note, only *some* women are capable of doing this, *not* all. There is also one

particular orgasmic response noted by Masters and Johnson, which they call 'status orgasmus', in which a few women are able to have a rapidly recurrent set of orgasms with no intermittent plateau phase at all. Women who experience this may be able to identify the different peaks or may simply feel they are going through an intensely long, drawn-out climax.

HELEN SINGER KAPLAN'S THEORIES

Some years later, Helen Singer Kaplan re-examined and rethought the sexual response cycle, building on the existing theory of Masters and Johnson. She categorised the phases of the cycle as *desire*, *arousal* and *orgasm*. What on earth does it matter, you may ask, since the outcome remains the same? But one of the important facts to emerge from Kaplan's observations is that although most women would hope to experience all three components of her cycle – desire, arousal and orgasm – these can each be experienced *individually* and are *not necessarily dependent on each other*. In other words, they do not have to occur in linear order. Apparently, we don't have to have the first phase in order to experience the second or third. Or even the second phase in order to experience the third.

The value of this to women with sex problems is that it gives us sex therapists a better idea of where things may be going wrong, which means we can develop more accurate methods of helping such women. It explains clearly, for example, the case of the woman who is able to masturbate to orgasm with a vibrator but who experiences no excitement of any kind while doing so, and very little sensation, apart from the feelings of contraction during orgasm. In

Kaplan's terms, this woman is cutting out the desire and excitement stages and simply experiencing orgasm. What is the cause of this? She is experiencing high levels of anxiety about her sexuality. In order for her to feel excitement and rather more of the climax, she needs to work on why she's anxious. The theory also explains the more common situation of the woman who feels the stages of desire and arousal but simply cannot get to orgasm.

Desire

This is a nebulous and difficult state to define. But put at its simplest, desire is the involvement of the brain at the beginning of the process of attraction. It is the feeling of desire that makes us pursue a love or sex object. It incorporates lust but may contain more than that pure animal sense, in that the attraction is (usually) focused on a particular human being. Many women who feel desire do not necessarily experience lust – at least to begin with. Many more do, however! The use of considering desire as part of the cycle is that if it is lacking, there are sex-therapy methods to encourage it.

Arousal

This is the equivalent of Masters and Johnson's excitement and plateau phase and covers the same ground. Kaplan considers the plateau phase as a component of excitement or arousal.

Orgasm

This is the equivalent of Masters and Johnson's orgasm and incorporates resolution as the natural consequence of orgasm.

There are further aspects that affect women's ability to respond sexually, such as particular hormones or special centres of sexuality in the brain; we will discuss these aspects more closely in Chapter 6.

THE G-SPOT

Something that women occasionally report is that they feel inhibited about climaxing because, when they do, they seem to urinate. If these women have had several children or have a complicated gynaecological history, the most likely cause of their urination is weakened or damaged bladder control. Accepting the fact and making good use of thick towels is the best solution here.

But once someone reported a very different experience. Lynette was a lesbian who knew she could climax because she managed it fine on her own, but who felt extremely inhibited when with a partner. She not only urinated when she came but did so in a jutting arc. This made her feel terribly ashamed.

It was very clear from Lynette's detailed description that she possessed an active G-Spot but didn't know it. What is a G-Spot? Its full name is the Grafenberg Spot, named after the German gynaecologist Ernst Grafenberg, and it is a sensitive area on the anterior wall inside the vagina. When pressed in the right way it triggers orgasm.

According to the researchers Dr John Perry, psychologist, and Beverly Whipple, nurse, every woman has a G-Spot. There is some dispute about this since clinical observation seems to show that only a few women possess one. I don't for a start. Part of the orgasm triggered by stimulating this spot can be a type of ejaculation. The women who took part in their laboratory tests sent out a fine spurt of fluid from their urethra during orgasm. And there is evidence on film documenting this.

What this substance may be, however, is controversial. Perry and Whipple insist that it is not urine but a substance that corresponds to seminal fluid (without the sperm). Other researchers, notably Daniel Goldberg who has analysed the fluid and insists that it is urine, dismiss this claim. The jury is out!

The most recent theory is that the spot, which feels to the fingers like a small bump, is the root of the clitoris where it juts into the vagina. Whatever it is, it certainly consists of some very richly endowed nerve endings. Vibrator manufacturers now make specific vibrator models that pulse against this upper vaginal area – on the grounds that it is pressure and pulsing rather than the up-and-down of fricative intercourse which sets off the G-Spot. Although everyone wants to know if they possess a G-Spot, it is of absolutely no concern if they discover that they don't.

Stimulating the G-Spot

This may be difficult to do to yourself because many women's fingers are not long enough to go far enough into the vagina to locate it. Some women find it easier to ask their lover to explore the upper vaginal wall for them. You are looking for a soft bump far back into the vagina on that upper wall. When you find it, try pressing it then letting go, pressing then letting go. We are not talking about a very hard pressure but more of a pulsation.

THE CLITORIS DURING LOVEMAKING

The clitoris plays a key role during sexual stimulation. It acts as both a receiver and transmitter of sexual feelings.

MYTH OF SEXUALITY

An old-fashioned misconception is that clitoris-size is related to the intensity of a woman's orgasm. In other words, the bigger the better. Masters and Johnson in their laboratory experiments have disproved this. It doesn't matter what size your clitoris is, your orgasm will be as good (or as bad) as anyone else's. Clinical observation, however, tends towards linking high amounts of the hormone testosterone with larger sex organs. This may not make any difference to the intensity of orgasm but it might make orgasm easier to experience.

INDIRECT CLITORAL STIMULATION

The way the clitoris becomes stimulated during inter-course is not usually by direct contact with the thrusting of the penis, since, anatomically, few of us are built so that the clitoris and penis encounter easily, but each time the penis thrusts in the vagina it exerts a pull on the labia. These, in turn, exert a pull on the clitoris. So, indirectly, the clitoris is being stimulated throughout intercourse.

This argues convincingly the case for the clitoral hood. In the 1960s there was a lot of publicity given to the 'hooded clitoris'; that which is so effectively hidden by the hood of skin over it that no stimulation can reach it. Surgeons used to operate on women to remove the hood, thus facilitating 'better sex sensation'.

In fact, there is only a microscopic percentage of

women who really need such an operation. They are the women whose hoods are attached with some kind of lesion to the clitoris and who therefore cannot pull back their pubic mound to expose the clitoris. (A male analogy would be the man who could not retract his foreskin because it had grown attached to the penis itself.) But these women are *exceedingly* rare.

For the rest the 'hooded clitoris' is a myth. What these women need is less thrusting and more masturbation. Usually when women can't find their clitoris, it's because they don't know it can be tucked up far inside the pubic mound. If you do need direct stimulation on the clitoris, therefore, no operations are needed. All you have to do is firmly but gently pull back the pubic mound and the clitoris will roll out from underneath.

Clitoral Jewellery

Ironically, the fashion in clitorises these days runs in totally the opposite direction, as it's now quite common for young women to wear clitoral jewellery fastened through a piercing in the clitoral hood. This is on the grounds that the movement of the jewellery stimulates them sexually.

HOW WOMEN MASTURBATE

Every woman masturbates in a way that is uniquely and individually her own. Some women stimulate the whole of their genital area and not the clitoris alone. This takes longer to climax but reputedly causes a stronger and more satisfying climax than by clitoral touching, and is less likely to be painful and irritating.

Some women find that the clitoris becomes painful when it has been manipulated too hard or for too long. They would perhaps react with more pleasure to very light fingertip circling and twirling on the apex of the clitoris. Very few women manipulate the head of the clitoris directly; most often they stimulate one side of the clitoral shaft. For the female orgasm to continue its full length, stimulation has to go on until the climax is completed. *It doesn't carry on, on its own, without continued stimulation.*

SIMULTANEOUS ORGASMS

It has been stated before now that simultaneous orgasms are an unnecessary goal, and Masters and Johnson say that observing oneself during intercourse ('taking a spectator role') can lead to impotence or female lack of orgasm. It's hard not to observe yourself if you are trying to time your orgasm to coincide with your partner's, so it does sound as though there is a certain danger for some people in aiming for this. However, there are many couples who have never found this a problem and love having simultaneous orgasms. Perhaps the best advice is that it doesn't matter in the slightest if you climax together or separately.

THE HOMEWORK DAILY SCHEDULE – WEEK FOUR

One hour a day.
Repeat the breathing, bio-energetics and Kegels exercises.

Day 1: Bath and self-massage. Genital massage as before.

Day 2: Continue with genital exploration. This time when you stop using your hands, experiment with your vibrator in the same way. If the vibrations are too strong and your clitoris is feeling oversensitive, try using the vibrator through a soft towel or a silk scarf. Try placing the vibrator on the entrance to the vagina, at the sides of the clitoris, at varying positions on the labia. Does it feel good if it is held very lightly over the clitoris, or is it better pushed against the clitoris very hard? Once more, don't aim at having an orgasm. You are simply trying to discover what kind of sensations you enjoy most in the genitals.

Day 3: Continue in the same way. Experiment with different pressures. Note down in your diary how you feel about this, if you feel any resistance to doing this, and how you think you might best overcome the resistance.

Day 4: As Day 2 but remember what has been said in the group about artificially heightened body excitement (page 38). See what deliberately tensing the pelvis, arching the back and breathing in a rapid and shallow way feels like.

Day 5: As Day 2. Bear in mind that ordinary vibrator batteries wear out rapidly. So if there is even a hint of less frequent vibrations, I suggest you change the batteries for new ones. Long-life batteries last longer and are also stronger. Alternatively, invest in a rechargeable battery kit. It might save you a fortune.

Day 6: Write your diary. Prepare for the group tomorrow. Make a list of SHOULDS/SHOULD NOTS.

SHOULDS/SHOULD NOTS

These operate in a similar way to the YES/NOs. Think carefully about what you feel you should or shouldn't do or be in your life and list them. These could be the 'I should be prettier therefore I'd better take more care of my appearance' or 'I should not be so fat therefore I'll go on a diet' sort of imperative or, interpreted on a more everyday level, 'I should be a better housekeeper, career woman' etc., right through to 'I'm fed up with the present government and therefore I should do something politically active to change things'. In other words, the SHOULDS/ SHOULD NOTS can be used on any level but whatever that may be, you will have to think carefully and conscientiously about them, and then hopefully do something about acting on your resolutions…!

FANTASIES

If you use any erotic fantasies that make you feel sexy, write them down and bring them with you to the next group meeting.

ADDITIONAL READING

How Big is Big? – The mysteries of Sexology Explained by Anne Hooper and Jeremy Holford (Robson Books, 2003). This is a history of sex research which gives a very clear idea of how our knowledge of sexual intimacy has developed.

SEX TOYS ONLINE

www.passion8.co.uk
www.sh-womenstore.co.uk
www.goodvibes.com (US store)

Chapter 5

WEEK FIVE

Summer is here. Outside the weather is bright and sunny and the women bring a reflection of these fine days into the flat. They are all wearing colourful dresses, even Maggie who usually sports blue jeans. Kate has caught up on her sleep, Maxie looks unusually smug and Haley is bubbling with gossip and energy.

In contrast to the early days, when at least someone would be late, today three of them are early. Jan, smiling and nodding, is swathed in floating flowered chiffons and Mary, as usual, is calm and composed, her long red hair flying free instead of pinned up in its usual knot.

As I said earlier, one of the first things noticeable during these group sessions is the gradual transformation in appearance and mood, throughout the weeks, which exactly matches internal psychological progress. Homework has generated good vibrations and judging from the happy faces, there have been more than a few.

TALKING ABOUT THE HOMEWORK

MAGGIE

'I have to confess I didn't do any more self-touching,' she tells us. 'I tried the vibrator the night of the last class. I couldn't resist it. I got back to my flat at about 11.30pm and my flatmates were all miraculously in bed. Just in case of disturbance, I locked the door and hung up my little notice. I didn't actually need it but I felt safer with it outside.

'I put the heater on even though it wasn't cold and curled up on my bed, warming the vibrator on my body. When I turned it on and heard the noise it made I went right under the bedclothes with it. It was so loud I thought it would wake up my flatmate.

'But she didn't come pounding on my door, so after a while, I managed to relax. I used the massage oil on my genitals to make them slippery and then I moved the vibrator up and down my labia like I would my fingers. After a while it felt so good on the clitoris that I concentrated there. I moved the vibrator ever so gently and lightly up and down the right side of my clitoris (that's where it felt best). And I had an orgasm, quite quickly. I *think* it was an orgasm.

'I got a few waves of nice feeling but they quickly finished. Then I remembered afterwards what you said about continuing the stimulation once the orgasms began, which is what I didn't do. I put the vibrator back again when I remembered but it was too late. The excitement wouldn't come back.'

'How many times have you used the vibrator?' I ask.

'I tried it twice more,' she replies. 'I did try keeping it on my clitoris longer each session, but – I don't understand why – I seem to move off unconsciously when I reach climax.'

'You sound as though you're blocking it out,' says Kate. 'You're nearly there but you're a bit scared of what's going to happen so your mind sends a message to the hand holding the vibrator and says "move off before we both blow up".'

'What should I do?' asks Maggie.

'Try and turn it into a YES/NO exercise. Tell yourself that if you're going to do it, there's no point unless you're prepared to give your body a decent chance. Insist on staying with the stimulation when you get to the confusing, explosive bit,' I suggest.

Maggie's mother has arrived to stay with her daughter. 'We talked for a long time last night. We've never really talked like two adults before. My mother has never previously breathed a word about how she feels about Dad. I told her about my fear of confronting him and all of a sudden she began to open up.

'It came out with a rush, pent-up, as if it's been bottled inside her for years. She finds him impossible, could never tell anyone because she thought she'd lose face. She's stuck it out all these years because of me. Now I'm not there she's asking herself what life is all about.

'I suggested she should leave him and her immediate reaction was panic. "What would I do?" she asked. "How would I live?" I suggested she ought to get some kind of retraining. "He'd never let me," she kept on saying. But I don't think that's true. I just don't think she's considered any alternative before.'

'How are you feeling about this?' asks Mary.

'Pretty upset,' she says. 'It's awful to think about how unhappy she is. But I also feel sorry for my Dad too. The sad thing is he has no idea how awful he is to live with. He just thinks that's how things should be between man and wife.

'But I still think, even if it's going to be scary, that Mum ought to try and start a life independently from him. If she feels leaving him is too much, she could at least get a job that would take her out of the house and give her some money of her own. So tomorrow I'm going to get online and find out details of retraining schemes. It can't hurt.'

HALEY

Haley has not enjoyed her vibrator. 'I was getting on far better with my fingers and with Len's fingers. It seems a more natural pace. The first time we used the vibrator I thought it was going to run away with me. It was terrifying. The second time, instead of getting me excited, I went numb. I wound up being unable to respond at all. I had to give myself a break of about twenty minutes before I could masturbate with my fingers instead.'

VIBRATOR VERSUS FINGERS

Some women are more stimulated by finger manipulation than by electrically-generated vibration. Haley may be one of them but it would be a mistake to discard the vibrator on the strength of having used it only twice. Haley agrees to try it a few more times in the next week. She also decides to try the vibrator through a layer of soft material. Numbness can be the result of too strong a vibration on a super-sensitive clitoris.

JAN

Everyone in the group has written down their SHOULD/SHOULD NOT exercise and most people's resolutions are similar. Jan's list includes 'I should not eat chips', 'I should be more decisive', 'I should learn to live alone' and 'I should not be afraid to make the first move in finding a man'.

Jan is still hovering on the brink of whether or not actively to go out and look for another boyfriend. Is it unfeminine to be so forward? Isn't that sort of behaviour unromantic?

Yes, debates the group, it *is* unfeminine in the old-fashioned sense, but so what? All the rules have changed over the past few decades. Young women are allowed to be the pursuers now if that's what they want. Many men *like* to be actively pursued. It's not only a compliment to them but it takes some of the responsibility for the first move off their shoulders. Why should it always be the men who are expected to do the running?

As for 'not being romantic', there are women aged 80 still sitting in the isolation of their family home waiting for Mr Right to come along and sweep them off their feet. It's much more fun to ring up Mr Right and ask him out. Saves about sixty years' waiting time.

Jan and her vibrator have taken to each other. Jan has never found it difficult to masturbate to orgasm. Her climax pattern is to become excited quickly, to reach orgasm easily, and then to have the excitement rapidly dwindle. Very occasionally she has climaxed twice in ten minutes, but this is not something that happens often.

With her new electric friend she finds she can have rapid multiple orgasms. 'Just as one is over,' she explains, 'another begins about five or ten seconds later. The first is a long one, then there's this series of shorter but extremely intense climaxes. Then, as the seconds go by, there are greater and greater gaps of time between each orgasm. I almost have to force the last one out. I quite consciously arch my body up to the vibrator for it.'

'What's Jim's reaction?' asks Maxie.

'He doesn't know I'm using the vibrator,' says Jan. 'I've only tried it out during the day. Mind you, he's not been in too much lately to see me. He's been spending more and more time round at his new girlfriend's place.'

'So it's not worth saying anything to him about it, then?' continues Maxie.

'No, I don't think so. Even if he takes another six months to move out, we don't have much left between us. Except Will, of course,' she adds wryly. 'At least Jim's been relatively quiet this week. Which means that Will and I are beginning to feel a little less tense.'

'Are you going to ask him to go?' Haley is curious.

'I don't have to do anything as formal as that. We've shouted and screamed so much about busting up and him moving out that it's pretty well understood to be on the cards. I'm just sorry *I* can't move out to speed things up. Since it's my flat I've got to stick it out. But don't worry, he'll go. There's no way we can go on living like this. He may not go tomorrow but he'll go eventually.'

I say, 'You're sounding very decisive now. Are you quite sure you are doing the right thing?'

'I think I've known we weren't going to work out for a long time. I was just too scared to do anything about it. But since I joined the group I can see that there are alternatives. And though he still has the ability to reduce me to jelly, I can harden up again afterwards. As long as I remember that, then I can cope.'

Maxie says, 'You've been coping for a long time already, if you ask me. You'll find things a whole lot easier once you've got your place back to yourself.'

MARY

Mary has had a hectic week of caring for her small children while preparing to move house. Her contract with Bruce is still holding out and she is feeling relief as a result.

'He's been working very hard this week,' she tells us. 'He comes home after a gruelling day at the office and launches into helping me pack up our belongings and paint the new house. He's been great. What constantly amazes me, though, is that even when he's exhausted he still wants sex. I'm sure I must have a far lower libido than he has. But he's been very nice this week and I've appreciated him. It's got nothing to do with sex, mind you.

'I think the new house is going to make a great difference. It's something for us to work on together, which we both enjoy. We won't be so overcrowded and it's got a garden, which is going to be fantastic for the children. For the past two years I've had children and nappies and a dog squashed into a tiny house in an area I don't like. I feel better just thinking about moving.'

One of Mary's SHOULD/SHOULD NOTS is 'I should remember Bruce is tired in the evening, therefore I should do more housework myself instead of relying on him' and another is 'I should show Bruce more affection'. Her use of the vibrator has been desultory. 'I don't feel I need it,' she says flatly. 'I don't feel right using it. I did try. But only for a couple of minutes, I admit. Mind you, having heard what you've just said to Maggie, I think I should give myself another go. A lot of my antagonism is due to prejudice. It's the same feeling I started off with about massage.'

KATE

Kate has been re-reading the Betty Dodson book *Sex For One*, and in particular has been looking at the drawings of female genitals. 'They are remarkable,' she says. 'She's made me feel a whole lot better about myself. I really thought my vulva was ugly and dirty, like a gaping wound. But now I begin to see the beauty, how flower-like a woman can appear. I was pretty unhappy about using the speculum before but I'm going to try again this week. I'm curious to have a better look at myself now.'

Kate *has* been using the vibrator, but although she has climaxed with it, she has developed certain fears.

VIBRATOR FEARS

'I've read that you can get hooked on a vibrator,' she says, 'Do you think that's true?'

If the alternative to being 'addicted' to a vibrator is to do without orgasms, I know which one I'd plump for. I've heard of women who have been unable to masturbate by hand after getting to know and love a vibrator, whereas I know of others who are happy to respond both to manual and electric accompaniment. Jo, my assistant, first learned to climax with a plain battery vibrator, subsequently learned to do it with her fingers, and eventually managed it in bed with her lover without any sexual aids. On the other hand, some women get set in their masturbation patterns and if they have become fixated on using a vibrator, may find it difficult to climax without it. But it is possible to change the pattern in which you masturbate (just as it's possible to learn how to climax), which means it is possible to be weaned from a vibrator to other methods of satisfaction.

Even though you may depend on a vibrator for sexual satisfaction, this does not mean you are limited to solitary, electric self-stimulation. It is very easy to take your vibrator to bed with a partner so that you both get pleasure and fun from it. Next week, we talk in detail about how to use the vibrator during lovemaking.

BISEXUALITY

Kate has been dying to ask Haley something for the last four weeks. Finally she plucks up her courage. 'I get turned on just by thinking of other women,' she tells us. 'In the dreams I've had when I've woken up having an orgasm, I've been watching a woman with very big breasts. I've often wondered if I might be bisexual.

'I feel very affectionate towards some of my girlfriends. When I did that massage with my friends, it was lovely to be able to massage Suzie, as well as my men friends. I liked having the opportunity to touch a woman. But I do have fears that if I actually made love to another woman, I'd never want to make love to a man again.

'What happened, Haley,' she asks, 'when you made love with a woman? How did you feel afterwards?'

Haley blushes. 'I met my friend socially, at a party. We got on so well that we each knew we were attracted to each other. It was like mental shorthand between us. We didn't talk much about it; we were instantly very close.

'I told Len how attracted I felt to her and he was very understanding. He told me that if I really wanted to get together with her, this was OK with him; he could empathise.

'Having virtually been given permission, I think my attraction and my curiosity were strong enough to make me do something about her. I invited my friend over to our house for supper one evening. And we went to bed together. It seemed a natural thing to do.

'Going to bed was pretty successful too. It was very exciting and very sexy, and I discovered I suddenly had a lot of insight into what turned men on. She enjoyed it; she could have orgasms very easily. I enjoyed it too but couldn't let go sexually in the same way. But I loved being with her and we met again a couple of times later and became great friends.

'Because I liked her didn't mean, though, that I lost all interest in men. I'm still very keen on Len. In fact, I like him better for allowing me to do something I needed to do. I don't think I'm a very representative bisexual, though. My main sexual friend is definitely Len. Jane is now a close friend, but the sexual curiosity has mostly died away. I think a real bisexual is someone who likes the opposite sex as much as they like their own sex.'

Sexuality Spectrum

The granddaddy of sexological research is the great Alfred Kinsey, who was the first person to codify the concept of sexuality as a spectrum. At one end is the very heterosexual person, interested only in the opposite sex. At the other end is the extreme homosexual, interested only in the same sex. Somewhere in the middle are the bisexuals, the exact centre being the 50/50 bisexuals. Kinsey argued that most of us fell into the middle spectrum with a greater or lesser degree of bisexuality. We may not know it. We may never do anything about exploring 'same sex' relationships, but that doesn't mean to say that we don't possess the capacity. At least, that's the theory.

Kate was relieved to hear that Haley had not apparently been overtaken by her desire for women to the extent of wanting to cut men out of her life.

'Nobody would force you to do that,' remonstrated Maxie. 'Nobody's going to make you do anything you don't really want to do.'

'You're right, of course,' says Kate, pulling a face.

'What's so terrible about finding out that you're a lesbian anyway?' asks Jan.

'There's so much social opposition to lesbians,' argues Kate. 'I'd be scared if I found out I was one.'

'Oh, for goodness sake,' says Jan. 'We've all moved on. No one gives a toss these days if you are lesbian, at least not if you live any kind of city life. I guess it might be different in the depths of the countryside. And if you really were a lesbian, loving a woman would seem much better to you than loving a man.'

'That's true,' she agrees. 'But it still doesn't stop it from being scary.'

'Anyway, it's OK to love women as well as men,' says Haley. 'And if you don't want to go ahead and love women, nobody's forcing you. You're a free agent, Kate.'

MAXIE

Maxie remains quiet until the last woman has spoken. But she has been talking a lot more than usual today although she hasn't, so far, contributed anything new about herself. This week she seems different. In the past she's sat around, elegant but solemn. Today she's smiling and moving, more awake and alert in the group than ever before.

'I didn't have time for my vibrator all week,' she tells us. 'I didn't use it till last night. I flounced into my flat at the end of the day in a stinking mood, exhausted and irritable, dumped my bags in the living room and went to the toilet.

'My toilet is in the bathroom and the vibrator was sitting on one of the bathroom shelves. In a fit of bad temper I picked it up and thought, "Oh, what the hell. I might as well." And tried it. In three minutes flat I had the most amazing multiple orgasm, out of nowhere. It was fantastic.' She finishes with the air of a showman, flourishing her arms.

Laughter and clapping come from the group. 'That's fantastic,' says Jan. 'Congratulations,' beam the others. 'Have you tried it again?' asks Haley.

'Not yet,' Maxie replies, smiling. 'But I'm dying to get home tonight.'

THE INFO

In the second half of tonight's meeting we talk about the use of fantasy in our sex lives and how menstruation may affect not only us and the way we react and feel, but also its influence on our husbands, children, partners and workmates.

FANTASY

Fantasy is still a relatively unexplored territory of our sexual lives for the obvious reason that it's not the easiest subject to quantify. How do you measure imagination?

Despite this, social scientists in past years have been gathering information about the relationship between sexual fantasy and body stimulation. One such researcher, Dr Glenn Wilson of the Institute of Psychiatry in London, has published a thought-provoking book on the subject, *The Secret of Sexual Fantasy*. In it he presents a number of facts and figures.

His findings indicate that the amount we fantasise is related directly to the strength of our sexual libido. But... if we have been conditioned against sexual feelings at some stage in our lives (as many of us have), the sex urge may be inhibited by feelings of guilt. And the feelings of guilt probably dampen down the fantasies. Certainly, many of the women who come to my groups have not previously experienced sexual fantasy.

So, just because you've never had fantasies, it doesn't necessarily mean you have a low libido. Nor does it mean you are unable to develop the ability to fantasise and the ability to experience orgasm. There are now many women who have been taught to be orgasmic by first of all turning on to erotic pictures or films, and second, by being encouraged to turn on to the memory of these. So it is possible to develop our sexuality through expanding the imagination. Interestingly, hand in hand with self-knowledge about the body's erotic responses goes a growth of the erotic imagination. The process is circular.

HILARY'S STORY

Hilary is a friend whose sex history illustrates wonderfully well the parallel growth of sexual experience and imagination. Hilary writes: 'I started off fantasising as a teenager and I suppose then my fantasies were based on reality. I would see a bloke in the street, fancy him and wonder what it would be like to go to bed with him.

'I would find myself picturing myself having sex with him. I think the proximity of the man had a lot to do with how I got turned on. I could do this with people I was talking to, standing close to. I would suddenly find I was off in a sexual daydream about him even while he stood there chatting in front of me. And I would have an orgasm. I didn't know it was an orgasm at the time. But I'd get waves of lovely feelings and a lot of tingly sensations. I'm sure, looking back, that they were orgasms and not just excitement.

'Much later, when I was about 23, I would climax during sex only if I was crazily in love. I felt these orgasms very much in my vagina. I was never aware of my clitoris being touched or even being involved in the sensations. It was very much to do with copulation. But I *had* to be madly in love. The less intense I felt, the less good were the feelings.

'I'd never really masturbated. I mean I had when I was about 13, with another girl. But that was just playing round. When we found a good spot, we thought, that's nice, so we hung around those good sensations. But I didn't know that we were masturbating. And I never did it with myself.

'When I started going to bed regularly with young men, at around 16 years old, I think I was as much in love with the art of sex as with sex itself. I used to think about it for three hours beforehand and build up to it in every way. I'd go through a whole ritual of rigorous perfuming and moisturising. Every inch of me, every orifice, would smell good and look good. In fact, looking good was a great part of it. If I knew I looked spotty and horrid, it wouldn't work. If I don't turn myself on I'm not capable of turning anyone else on.

'I think all this preparation had a lot to do with my insecurity. I was very unconfident then. Had to build up my ego to go into the fray. But also the ritual of the preparation was a kind of fantasy for me. It would work me up and make me sexy.

'With Richard I was in love for the first time in an adult way. I couldn't wait to leap into bed with him. And when I got there we were immediately very sexual. There didn't have to be such a great build-up. For the first time I had great waves of orgasmic feeling, really marvellous. I didn't fantasise with him at all. I must have been 18 years old.

'I often couldn't see him for a very long time. And I missed him very much. I'd got married at that stage to someone else. I simply couldn't get tuned into my husband's lovemaking at all. He was far too aggressive and matter-of-fact about it. I'd lie awake for hours beside him in bed, missing Richard violently. And that's when I began to fantasise. Without moving a muscle (I couldn't for fear of waking up my husband), I'd remember all the very sexy incidents with Richard and I'd come. Without touching myself or moving any part of me, I'd have a climax.

'Those orgasms started right in the brain. A hot liquid feeling would shoot down me. I'd be very moist between the legs and feel very hot on the outer lips. Waves of delicious feeling would go through me. I'd feel most of it in my stomach and vagina. It would be as though the mental action of my fantasy would get taken over by the physical action of my body.

'I didn't do this only in bed, either. I used to do it, quite involuntarily, standing in a public queue.

'I eventually left my husband, not for Richard, who was married, but for Parker. To begin with we played a lot of sex games but then he got to telling me stories in bed. He'd start by telling a story about something sexual and in the story the something sexual would be happening to me. I'd get really turned on by this and eventually we'd move on to intercourse but he would carry on with the story at the same time. He's got a great imagination.'

Hilary is aware that her fantasies grow and expand out of each other. She isn't remotely bothered about the fact that in some of her fantasies she is abused, used and masturbated by men she finds gross and unattractive. She says she wants to feel like this *in her dream life*. In reality, though, she's a strong, forceful character who, if truly used and abused, would react with anger.

Hilary's comments about the fantasies she experiences when using her vibrator are useful to hear because they are a good example of how fantasy can help create a really powerful and imaginative sexual experience.

'One fantasy is about me making a blue movie. There are a lot of people involved in making this film, all watching from shadowy corners around the set. It starts with my making a deal, fixing the price, going into the business details.

'We start the movie. And once I get really excited I'll do anything. I'm out of control, not in command of my actions any more. And the film men can see that I'll do anything and they start making suggestions, more and more outrageous suggestions, and each time, the crazier the things are the more excited I become. Until I come.

'I don't think I'd ever act out any of my fantasies. I've often wondered how I would feel if I did. Would I get as turned on in real life? I'm sure I wouldn't. I do know that from being a teenager who thought she was frigid and never came, I've learned through using my imagination that I'm highly sexed. I have two or three orgasms a day. Which is incredible when I think of the years of marriage where I remained sexually dead.'

SURE-FIRE FANTASIES
The reason I've recounted Hilary's story in such detail is because once the novelty of successful masturbation has worn off a little, it sometimes gets harder to climax again. This is where the value of fantasy comes in. If you can

learn to use fantasy either by dreaming up your own or, failing a fertile imagination, by reading about somebody else's, you can spur yourself on to an easier climax.

Very often the women in my classes haven't considered fantasising before and don't know where to start. One of the best and most original books of women's fantasies is *My Secret Garden* by Nancy Friday, first published in 1973 and still available today. Fortunately, these days there's also a small army of erotic writers spinning out volumes of sexual stories, which you can find with a quick browse of the sex titles on Amazon.

One of the pieces of homework that the group does is to write down their favourite fantasies and bring them along to the group. What follows is a selection, including one borrowed (with permission) from Nancy Friday.

KATE (on whom the character of Kate in this book is partly based)

'I'd like to write my fantasies in three stages because I think it's very interesting how they changed as a result of coming to the workshop.

Stage 1: 'Before coming to the pre-orgasmic group, I only experienced orgasm as the result of a dream and I could come in the night as a result. Always a woman appeared, sometimes standing behind a window. I would look in, she would take her clothes off and, on seeing her breasts, I would wake and have an orgasm.

Stage 2: 'Since starting the workshop I have stopped coming in this way – no more dreams of women and no more waking up to have an orgasm, with one exception: during the first part of the course I became very conscious of the way I was allowing my boyfriend and people at work to dominate me. I told my boyfriend (and more important, acted on it) that either he decided we get together or we quit. I then had a dream in which I was facing the problem of telling a colleague at work – I was her 'senior' – that she could not have her holiday at the time she wanted. (This was a problem in real life.) She began to complain. I then physically experienced a very powerful contraction in my vagina and woke up with orgasms! The next day, effortlessly, I told my colleague what the situation was on this issue.

Stage 3: 'In conscious, waking life I can now fantasise, and with the help of a vibrator, in such a way that it brings me to orgasm. In my fantasy I'm in the changing room at the squash club. Suzie comes in, my boyfriend Ian's ex-girlfriend. We are close friends in real life. She begins to undress – she's very bosomy – and another friend of mine, Mike, comes in too. He's tall, dark with thick curly hair. He is exposing himself, showing a large erection. I then come to orgasm.

'A slight development of the above is in Mike's sitting room, where he's entertaining Suzie and me. I get up and encourage Suzie to kneel in front of Mike who's sitting on the sofa. Standing behind Suzie I take off her top slowly still looking at Mike – he's transfixed by both of us. Slowly I begin to caress Suzie. Mike begins to undress. He has an enormous erection and I come immediately to orgasm.'

VIVIAN (from *My Secret Garden* by Nancy Friday)
'I had this fantasy the very first time I had sex. Jimmy was the first man for me. He's still the only one, but no matter

who I sleep with later on, I think I'll always have these thoughts abut Jimmy. They just seem to automatically spring to mind whenever I open my legs.

'Anyway, that first night, I don't think we slept very much... Maybe the second or third time that night he put me into this position; I think it's the position that inspired this idea in the first place, the idea that I was being planted. I was lying on my back, all my weight on my shoulders, with my legs straight up and over his shoulders. He was high above me – I remember looking up and seeing him looming large over me and coming down into me, boring down on me. Straight down into me. Not a frightening picture – on the contrary, I felt very large and accommodating, very wide and open, waiting for him to fill me up with his thrust. Waiting for him to plant seed like I was a large, warm, fertile hole in the earth, just for him, for that purpose, to be planted... In fact, I was all hole, and he, he was like some great harvest planting machine moving down the field, me, moving from hole to hole with each thrust. And I was all the holes; I was the earth. I was planted again and again. It was so exciting...to be planted by an earth planting machine, his enormous harvester that could plunge deeper into the earth than anything, could fill me up and leave me planted, ripe...that was it, I suppose; not just the excitement of being planted, but of knowing that with each thrust, I would be left whole, complete. Can you understand that? It wasn't the machine that was exciting – though the inexorable size of it was. What was exciting was the seed part. Or me being the earth. God, I don't know...but I love that feeling.'

LINDA

'I'm not too hot on fantasies. Maybe my imagination doesn't work that way. My major fantasy is of swimming in clear blue water (sea – not lakes) under a brilliant sky. My husband and I attempted lovemaking in just such a situation once; maybe it was because there was no tension, because expectations of success were so low, that I now see it as the ideal.

'A friend of mine dreams of being stroked with oil, grease, anything slimy, and she does say that it helps her reach orgasm if her boyfriend smothers her in grease beforehand.

'It also helps me just to think about the orgasmic experiences – to imagine what I will feel during orgasm and to imagine myself being made love to.'

HANNAH

Hannah has always wanted to be an actress and does a lot of amateur work, but she is too shy to audition for a professional role. She is unmarried and currently lives with an aspiring actor who is 'just a good friend'.

'My main problem is that I never have quite enough courage to do the things I really want to do. Same with men – I never go after the ones who really turn me on; instead, I stick with men who are harmless and devoted. But my fantasies are another story! My favourite fantasy scenario I call "The Audition" and I think of it whenever I want to turn myself on.

'In it, I am an all-powerful figure – bold, arrogant, slightly cruel, and hard to please. It begins with dozens of men being sent up to audition for me. I am reclining on a

couch, languidly watching them go through their paces.
The purpose? To see who will have the immense good
fortune to be my bed partner that night! A male secretary
waits in the wings to usher in each new candidate. I
dismiss one after another with a curt "Next!"

'Finally, in comes an adorable – and very nervous –
creature. I let him wait while I jot down a few brief
impressions. This gorgeous man is dressed in very tight,
bleached-out jeans and a soft white shirt unbuttoned a
little so that I can see the caramel-smooth skin of his chest.
He has tiny hips and a lovely, small bottom outlined
perfectly by the thin materials of his jeans. I ask him to turn
around – appreciating the play of muscles in his ropy
thighs as he pivots slowly – and then to recite his vital
statistics, including the size of his penis.

'This makes him blush, but I am very businesslike. I
order him to strip slowly. By the time he's down to his tiny
briefs, I have to admit that he's perfect. As he begins to
peel them down, I call out sharply: "I want you to lower
them very slowly. Try to excite me – think about what
you're doing."

'He tucks his thumbs in his briefs, inclining his pelvis
slightly – rocking it in slight, undulating movements – and
teasing the material down a millimetre at a time.

'First I get a glimpse of his curly, blond pubic hair, and
then a tantalising view of the beginnings of his prick. He
slips his hands down and allows his strong, tapering
fingers to caress the outer edges of his tense thighs,
making cupping motions to emphasise and frame the
swelling bulge.

'"Nice, very nice," I say professionally. "Before you

show me what you've got, tell me what you'll do to me if you're chosen."

'Stammering, he tells me how much he wants to make love to me, to lick me from my toes to the nape of my neck.

'Finally he pulls his briefs all the way down and his penis catapults out, fully erect and straining out towards me, rock-hard and sort of...pleading. I can see a pulse beating in his groin as he stands before me; a small groan escapes his lips and it looks to me as if his knees will buckle if I don't do something quickly.

'"All right," I say briskly. "You've been selected. Be back at nine tonight." Then he's taken off to a recovery room until his erection subsides.

'In this scenario, I remain cool and collected but the *real* me – the one imagining all this – is almost at the brink of climax just fantasising about it...'

Since fantasies are like dreams, they cannot really be resisted, although I have shown that they can be encouraged. Any woman can find herself, despite herself, thinking about erotic situations at any moment in her life. She may try and forget this. But why should she? Sexual fantasies are not 'policeable': they can't be 'correct' or 'incorrect', because they are not real.

Fantasies can represent doubts, fears and suppressions of ourselves as often they represent aspects of our true, conscious selves. People can be aroused by imaginary behaviour, which in their waking lives they would completely reject. Why this is so complicated and not fully understood is still a puzzle. But fantasies may be extended and enjoyed simply for their pleasurable by-product –

enhancing both your own sex life and through *your* enjoyment, your partner's too. Just as it would be illogical to feel guilty about your dreams, it is also illogical to feel guilty about your imagination.

You are *not* 'cheating' on your partner by thinking of another situation or person during lovemaking. You are bringing part of your being into play – your brain. And by doing this you are enriching your sexual experience. Successful sex in a relationship contains a selfish element, as we discussed in Chapter 1. Nobody else can have your orgasm for you. This is a private moment in your own consciousness. Similarly, lovemaking means surrendering to sex itself, including sexual thoughts, as well as accepting and initiating the embraces of a lover.

MENSTRUAL CYCLE

Not only are there phases in our lives when we find it hard to turn on, due to past inhibitions and present guilty feelings, but in addition, being women we can be subject to a constant monthly turmoil of emotions. For, along with the monthly menstrual *body* cycle, goes a monthly *emotional* cycle. Many women experience a peak of sexual desire at and around menstruation and many experience another peak around the time of ovulation (roughly the middle of each cycle).

Of course, there have been many taboos in the past against having sex at the time of menstruation, based on religious beliefs and practices. Women have therefore been taught to think of themselves as repellent at the time of their flow of blood (literally unclean). Not unnaturally, any sexual feelings on their part at such times have often been repressed.

If, however, instead of marking off the 'monthlies' as a no-sex time, we do the opposite and begin to develop them as a best-sex time, some delightful and sensual experiences may be the result. For this is not only a phase of increased body-sensitivity, but also an emotional peak. Of course, it is also a period of clumsiness and sometimes increased accident-proneness, but in the past it was only these negative qualities that were focused on. It may be of far-reaching importance to understand that the time around menstruation (the *paramenstrum*) can be the most creative, sensitive and sensual passage of the month.

One method of understanding your own unique cycle of physical and emotional wellbeing on a monthly basis is to keep a regular diary of moods and healthiness – a menstruation diary.

HOW TO KEEP A MENSTRUATION DIARY
Record daily:

- your moods
- physical feelings (whether you are tired, energetic, feel sexy or feel ill)
- your dreams
- your fantasies
- body changes
- sexual activity

By doing this, not by the calendar month but by the menstrual month, it is possible to draw a chart of where to

expect your moods and activities to lie on future days of
the month.

ANNE'S DIARY

I tried it out myself as an experiment. Here I reproduce
some excerpts from my diary.

PARAMENSTRUM
Thursday 5 January. Day 24 Feel as though my face is
bloated because my eyes are trying hard to see from
underneath puffed-out eyebrows. My mood in the morning
is sleepy and I remember vaguely dreaming something
complicated about sex therapy in the office. In the
afternoon, after a hard day's work, I find myself becoming
rapidly enraged and hostile, focusing on one particular
member of the staff, who is being particularly offensive.

I'm aware, however, that my symptoms are extremely
premenstrual. Nevertheless, I'm in such a rage on my way
home that I reach crisis point. Having done that, I float free
of the anger and start being constructive with my thoughts
and feelings about work. I go through alternate rages and
moments of calm, setting my life to rights for an hour and
a half. Anyway, by eleven o'clock, although I still have the
puffy-eyes feeling and know I'm tired, I've done a good
day's work. Totally unsexual, I go to bed and fall asleep
over my book.

Friday 6 January. Day 25 Am woken by a phone call.
Am instantly awake and charming to friend. On putting
down phone am extremely loving and cuddly with rather
closer friend. In sharp contrast to yesterday, this morning
I'm relaxed, clear-eyed, fresh, feeling like work, feeling

alive and I'm sensual. Can't tear myself away from lovely man. Could quite happily stay stroking and cuddling him all day long. Feelings of *joie de vivre* and sensuality remain all day. While I'm typing this, shortly after work, I'm wondering how I can lure my man into bed. He's been talking about needing exercise and going for a run. Perhaps, instead, if I casually wandered into the kitchen…? So much energy whirling inside me.

Saturday 7 January. Day 26 and, as it turns out, Day 1
We made love last night, not on my part from a compulsive need to do it, but because we sort of drifted into it. In fact, to begin with, I wasn't even sure if I wanted to. But once we'd begun, I was very glad because I was in one of those marvellous physical states where all my sensations were velvet. Anywhere I touched, and any touch I put out to him, felt floating and exquisite. Each bit of my flesh was full of tiny air bubbles, all receiving stroking delight. I didn't orgasm in the end, because it would have taken too long. I really could have stayed being stroked and touched all night. Marvellous.

Discovered in the morning why I'd felt so sensual. My period began two days early. If someone could market whatever it is that floats through my body the night before a period, they'd be the world's greatest millionaire.

Still slightly tetchy, but not so much. And it alternates with great feelings of love for Phillip. Perhaps if we could make love all day throughout the days immediately at the beginning of a period, I'd do away with all premenstrual snappiness.

The blood speeds up through the day, until in the evening it's flowing fast. I'm very tired by nighttime but find it hard to sleep – my body doesn't feel really comfortable and Phillip's movements wake me up once or twice.

Sunday 8 January. Day 2 Body is tired but I'm using my early-morning energy to work. This afternoon I'll flake out. Blood flowing fast still and I'm a little achy. I do have a desire this weekend for walking. Did a lot of it yesterday and would like to again this afternoon. I don't normally get this urge. I don't feel particularly sensual today, though I suspect that's because such a great part of me wants to work. Which cuts out the time I want to spend in bed. Later, later…

In fact, not at all. Come bedtime I was totally off sex, to the point of feeling thoroughly fed up when he wanted to make love. The sweet thing I discovered, halfway through, was that he was only doing it for me. We gave up. Thoroughly exhausted. Got a bit tearful again but it didn't last. Not like yesterday, which I forgot to mention, but for some reason I cried my head off.

LEADING UP TO OVULATION TIME

Tuesday 17 January. Day 11 I'm exhausted all day from my paltry sleep and fall into bed, demanding (successfully) to be read out loud to, which does a lot to make me feel better about Phillip. I sleep, although he awakes in a sweat every two hours.

Wednesday 18 January. Day 12 In the morning we give away the remains of our frozen Cornish catch (last night's indigestible fish) to a friend. I make a point of saying "Don't wake me up when you come to bed" – aware that Phillip is going to do his turning up at two in the morning routine, after reading in the bath. I'm defiant about my sleep and desperately tired. I felt totally unlustful last night, although I suspect he was sexy. I wonder if it's the mind turning the body off on purpose, because, later in the night, I woke and sleepily masturbated.

Sunday 22 January. Day 16 I'm woken at nine o'clock this morning by my dreams.

OVULATION TIME?
Monday 23 January. Day 17 My discharge changes to a brownish-red stain. Does this mean I'm ovulating now? I'm certainly dreaming a lot. I woke this morning with fragments of three dreams rushing through my head, concerning my work and the people I meet there.

Phillip points out that it's the full moon tonight. Perhaps that is the cause, he suggests, of my restlessness and generally nasty mood today. It certainly has been a bad, jerky sort of day. I've been out of sorts, wanting to burst into tears, unable to cope with being hassled at work and overcome by an engulfing sub-editing job. Totally sexless in addition.

Tuesday 24 January. Day 18 I'm not much better today. I'm a bit jollier but very tired. I do manage to relax with the kids in the afternoon, but for the rest of the day, I'm on edge. P says it's because I haven't had any sex. He could be right, but I refuse him again tonight.

Wednesday 25 January. Day 19 Calming down somewhat although I'm still tired, but then I *have* been slaving over my office work and it's been draining me.

Thursday January 26. Day 20 I have a manic energy, which whisks me through a very busy day. I am, needless to say, when I crawl into bed, dog-tired. My climax turns out to be frighteningly strong tonight. It's so strong that momentarily I block it off, cutting out the feelings. But then I force myself to unblock and let that incredible vibrant strength shake my whole body and I scream as loudly as I can. Thank heavens Bobby's no longer in the next room. And it's scary. P too is pretty rampant and comes strongly himself. Of course, none of this force is surprising since this is the fifth day since we've fucked and speaking for myself, I've only masturbated once in that time. Obviously one's sex energy stores up as in a generator and is only released when it's used.

In the past months, through continuing this kind of detailed self-monitoring, I've discovered that, regular as clockwork, I begin a heavy stringy discharge on Day 12. Around Day 16 and 17 I become exhausted for exactly 48 hours, in the meantime experiencing a slightly dis-coloured discharge possibly tinged with blood. During this fatigue I sleep uncomfortably and dream incessantly (I assume I am ovulating). As I reach Day 25 and onwards I'm tetchy and irritable but I'm beginning to feel sexier. The night before my period is sexual magic and I'm drumming with creative energy. From Day 1 to Day 12 I'm sexy. Then, once again, with the onset of the Day 12 discharge, my easy sexuality switches off like a time clock. Which has put my ego in its place because I honestly thought of myself, previously, as being sexy all the time. Instead, rather too often, I'm irritable, moody and unsensual. Oh dear!

DIFFERING LIBIDOS

One of the reasons women come to pre-orgasmic workshops is because their partners object to their lack of interest in sex. Of course, if there is a marriage of someone with a high libido to someone with a low libido, there are going to be discrepancies. For although both partners are 'normal', those libidos won't match up.

There are several reasons why sex drives range from high to average to low. We now know that the hormone *testosterone* plays a great part in deciding this. Women also possess testosterone, albeit in much smaller quantities than men. It appears to be testosterone that designates sexual response, drive and sensual experience. Some women are born with a lot, some women possess a little and most of us fall somewhere in between.

But inhibition can also dampen sexual desire, far more notably in women than in men (see Chapter 6, Physical Solutions, for more explanation). In the context of the menstrual cycle, however, the cycle itself can make desire fluctuate from one week to the next.

Everyone's monthly cycle varies. Although for about two-thirds of *my* cycle I don't feel very sexy, I am capable of having an orgasm *provided the stimulation is stepped up*. But it becomes much harder than in the lovely sensitive days of Day 1 to 12. Anorgasmic women – eighteen per cent of women, according to a sample in *The Hite Report* by Shere Hite – are in a permanent state of 'not feeling sexy'. What they don't know, because they have never found it easy to climax, is that they are probably capable of it, provided they persevere and provided they *increase the stimulation*.

Thus, not only may a particular woman's libido differ from her mate's but, in addition, it can differ in itself from week to week. What is the answer? Is it 'natural' and 'right' to accept that you are unlikely to climax? Or is it advisable to change over to what some people once called 'unnatural', that is, self-stimulation?

Since I know it's in *my* nature to enjoy some delightful lovemaking during the 'unsexy' days and, with a little perseverance, to experience some poignant orgasms, I would think it is more than OK to bring about a change. Happily, nothing appalling has happened to my health after thirty years of an active sex life.

So, to those women who've not yet enjoyed a climax and to others who think they have a low libido, the message reads: *you can intensify your sexuality if you want to*. And one of the easiest ways to do that is by making use of a vibrator or a fantasy.

THE HOMEWORK DAILY SCHEDULE –
WEEK FIVE

One hour a day.
Repeat breathing, bio-energetics and Kegels every day.

Do bath/self-massage when you can and then go on to masturbation practice. If you want to pursue the self-stimulation by hand, give yourself at least thirty minutes on it. If you get bored or fed up, take a short break and then carry on. (It takes some women up to an hour of continuous stimulation to reach orgasm at first.)

If you feel you are getting nowhere with the manual masturbation, experiment with the vibrator. How do you feel about using it? If last week you already used the vibrator, continue noticing the pattern of your sexual response, noting down any queries to discuss in the group.

ADDITIONAL READING

My Secret Garden by Nancy Friday (Pocketbooks, 1973). This book is a seminal collection of sexual fantasies contributed by real women in the US and UK.

The Secrets of Sexual Fantasy by Dr Glenn Wilson (Dent, 1978). No longer in print but copies still available through Amazon and AbeBooks. Also in public libraries. It provides a fascinating description of sexual fantasies and how these may effect our sexual persona.

The Wise Wound by Peter Redgrove and Penelope Shuttle (Marion Boyars, 2005). This is a poetic, psychological and literary powerhouse explanation of how menstruation has influenced the way the world views women, throughout the ages.

Chapter 6

WEEK SIX

Week Six is a celebration and a farewell. Jo's tabby cat winds his way among the glasses on the floor. We're having a festive drink to say goodbye.

Although it's finishing-off time for the group, Kate, Haley, Maxie and Jan are already making plans to continue meeting. Before we get down to our goodbye massage, though, there are a few pleas for help. Unprecedented, Maxie speaks first.

TALKING ABOUT THE HOMEWORK

MAXIE

'I've been so thrilled with the vibrator,' she tells us, 'that I've tried it every night. And it's getting harder and harder to come. It was lovely to begin with but on the third night I took much longer to get excited. On the fourth and fifth night it either took hours and then the climax didn't feel very good, or I gave up altogether. Why? What's happened?'

'Sounds as though your body is working out its natural sexual pace,' I venture. 'Maybe you're not someone who needs immense multiple orgasms every night. Maybe, if you only used the vibrator every third night, you'd leave your body enough time to recharge its sexual batteries.

'On the other hand, it may be that you are beginning to get used to the vibrator and that once it's no longer a novelty you need an added stimulus.'

'Such as a fantasy?' suggests Kate, who has used some of this herself.

'Or new batteries,' offers Haley. 'They wear out incredibly fast.'

'Or possibly a bit of both,' says Maxie. 'Did anyone else find this happened?'

MAGGIE

Maggie shakes her dark head in an emphatic cloud of no. 'I tried building up the excitement and then stopping, then beginning again. And I gave myself hours. When I did finally get to a strong peak of excitement I carried on with the vibrations and held the feeling right there. I didn't take the vibrator off this time and although it felt very weird and confused, I did come. It wasn't at all what I expected. I've been expecting this cascade of marvellous feeling. And instead it was like a motor turning over a few times before it died again. It was OK, but I found it disappointing. I thought it would be much better than it was.'

'But you've done marvellously,' cries Haley. 'Like last week you couldn't even let yourself stay with the vibration. That's fantastic. This week you've actually allowed yourself to go over into an orgasm. That's wonderful progress.'

'I expect you simply need to practise,' says Jan. 'It sounds as though you're being very tentative over letting yourself come. At least you've begun. When you get used to the sensations, you'll probably let yourself go a little more each time. And when you do, your orgasm will come out a bit stronger each time.'

'Try and open yourself up to the sensation,' suggests Haley. 'Try to abandon yourself to the feelings, instead of trying to fight them. Throw yourself into the jumble and confusion. I know it can be a bit frightening, but nothing terrible will happen to you.'

'I'm frightened of losing consciousness,' Maggie admits. 'That's what I feel might happen. I'm frightened of actually passing out. I've read that some women do.'

'Some men do too,' says Mary. 'My husband did the very first time he had sex with anyone.'

'It's a fear of losing control, isn't it?' I contribute. 'But as we've said earlier [Chapter 4], when you climax you only momentarily lose control and move into a different consciousness. A very few people on rare occasions do faint, but that tends to be only when they are at an extreme of excitement. It is highly unlikely you will lose complete consciousness, Maggie. You *will* be focused inwards to the exclusion of what's going on around you. Doesn't mean that you will faint, though.'

'It's getting over that fear that's going to help, isn't it?' Maggie muses.

'If you carry on using the vibrator and getting familiar with it, you'll probably find the fear goes away of its own accord.'

'What happened with your mother?' asks Jan.

Maggie brightens up. 'She went back to Dad yesterday. She doesn't really want to leave him, in spite of everything. But she's got really enthusiastic about actually going out and doing something. We did investigate some of the retraining schemes, but in the end she got very interested in going back into education. She thought doing something like a degree at the Open University would fit in with her life. It would give her the opportunity to slowly start meeting new people and doing new things. Much better than the shock of being plunged into something completely new, like a job or a full-time course. She's been at home for 27 years. It's a long time. It must be scary for her to begin something new. The OU will ease her in gradually. She looked much happier when she went back home, simply from having thought of an alternative to the miserable life she's been leading so far.'

She pauses for an instant, looks a little shy and then speaks again. 'I made a decision too. I decided that if, at the end of the summer, I didn't have a better job or a new boyfriend, that I would go out to India where my boyfriend is, providing of course that he still wants me to go out.'

'I thought you didn't want to go out there,' puzzles Mary.

'I didn't want to two years ago,' Maggie admits. 'But I feel now I'd like to see a country other than my own. I'll be scared by the travelling but also very interested in it.

'The other reason I didn't go two years ago was because I didn't really think Joe wanted me. He was scared he would become totally responsible for me, trapped into marriage if you like. And now, I think I could go over, look after myself and if it didn't work out between him and me, I know I'm capable of getting back on my own. I feel a lot more confident than I did before. If he's willing to take the risk of having me over there, then I'm willing to take the risk of going.'

MARY

Having tried the vibrator yet again, Mary has decided she definitely prefers being aroused by herself or by her husband, using fingers.

'I suppose because we're in the throes of moving house we've reached a stage in our lives where we're re-evaluating everything. Partly because I can actually climax now, but mostly because we don't have to make love so often, our love life as a result is getting better. We had a long talk the other night. We resolved that with our move we are going to make our lives freer. Once we're settled into the house we're going to give each other a lot more time off. We'll arrange it so that each can spend time separately from the other, nights away even, and that's going to be OK. It means we can have other lovers if we choose and it'll be acceptable to both of us.

'Sounds great, doesn't it! Whether or not it'll work, I've no idea. But the way Bruce talked about it, I think he can cope with it and I'm sure I can.'

'Aren't you afraid that one of you will fall in love with someone else?' asks Haley, appalled. 'Suppose that happens?'

'If it does happen we'll have to cope with it when it arrives. I don't think it will, though, because he's so blown away by me and I think he's a great husband and a great friend. I know my pattern with lovers and even if I do fall in love, the love fades away after a time.

'Bruce is a great husband for me. I value him very much. I value him particularly for coming to this kind of an agreement with me. There can't be many men who would do that. It would be very, very hard for me to meet up with someone who is going to be better than Bruce as a long-term prospect. And there's no point in my suddenly changing my life for any lover. I know that the odds are I'd lose interest in him after a few months. It just seems to be my pattern.'

'Rather you than me, friend,' says Jan. 'I find it hard enough concentrating on one person, let alone two. Aren't you going to find your life terribly split up?'

Mary ponders this. 'I've never found the slightest problem with that when I've been having affairs before. The only difference now is that I'm going to be able to be open about them instead of deceitful.

'Look, if in time the arrangement turns out to be an awful mistake, we'll rethink it. We've discussed all this and we have gone into the problems. We're both more confident people now and therefore I think much more able to carry it off.'

JAN

'I'm sitting on totally the other side of the fence,' says Jan. 'All I want to do is to settle down with the man of my dreams and live happily ever after. Meanwhile, the man of my nightmares is still living in my flat, muttering dire threats of retribution. I thought he'd gone last week because a lot of his stuff disappeared, but he returned a day later. I'm feeling surprisingly OK about him, mostly because I'm having such an amazing time with my vibrator. It doesn't have rows with me and it's such an accurate lover!'

'We've thought up a lovely dating ad for Jan,' Maxie tells us. 'The minute Jim finally gets out she's sending it off. We spent last night egging each other on and getting up enough courage to write it.'

'All I've got to do now,' says Jan, 'is hope that someone nice will answer. In fact, Maxie doesn't know it, but I actually took the plunge this morning and e-mailed it off.'

We all giggle and speculate about who might respond.

HALEY

'I tried using the vibrator through a silk scarf,' she tells us, 'to see if it felt any better. It did. I came and it was quite nice, but I really prefer using my fingers. It's something both Len and I have got good at now, and it just feels sexier somehow. Fingers just turn me on much more. So we've decided to stick with them for the time being and use the vibrator occasionally. There's nothing especially new to report. Len and I are getting on very well. He's delighted by the masturbation and I'm feeling particularly happy with him.'

KATE

'I've had mild orgasms with my vibrator,' she tells us. 'It doesn't seem to be so effective as before somehow. I've been using it with some of Ian's magazines, which turn me on a lot. But it's getting harder to come.'

'This sounds like the time for a reminder,' I say. 'The batteries run down very rapidly in battery-charged vibrators. You must remember to change them often.'

Jan giggles. 'The man at our local hardware shop can't understand what I keep buying these batteries for.

He's started to ask. It's getting difficult to avoid an explanation.'

'Ever heard of bulk buying?' says Haley. 'That would solve the problem.'

'The vibrator slows down when the batteries are low,' I continue. 'And the slower it gets, the harder it is for you to achieve orgasm.'

'How are things with Ian?' Haley asks Kate.

'Not so good. He finds it hard to accept my attempts at independence. He won't listen to the theory behind them. And he's shown no interest in the vibrator at all. I've wanted to use it with him but he's been very heavy-handed and I can see that he's bored silly. None of which is particularly aphrodisiac. And he sends me into a towering rage which doesn't help things at all!'

Kate's problem with Ian is a natural lead-in to the second half of our discussion on the subject of how to combine vibrators with more traditional lovemaking.

THE INFO

MAKING LOVE TOGETHER

Hopefully, by Week Six, most members of the group have learned how to make love to themselves. They know by now which strokes of the fingertips and which vibratory pressures can turn them on *enough* to give them an orgasm.

Once this is the case, the next step, for those women who want to, is to bring this new-found knowledge into their relationships. The first move is to get the message across to their lover that by learning to masturbate his/her partner he/she can give maximum sensual pleasure. It's a good idea to give up sexual intercourse entirely and concentrate only on learning to bring each other to climax by hand. It's what most teenagers used to do in the olden days when petting was OK but intercourse was not – the days before reliable contraception.

HOW TO HELP YOUR LOVER

The greatest difficulty here is not just that your partner might be 'doing it wrong' but in getting him or her to understand how to 'do it right'. It is of course desperately hard to give sex instructions when you are fearful; your partner may be discouraged by them and you may be worried that, as a result, he/she will eventually reject them and you. This is where the assertion exercises prove vital. You have everything to lose by not being brave enough to persist with your explanations and instructions, and nothing to gain if you are chicken and keep quiet.

If your partner really cares about you, he/she wants to hear your preferences, wants to learn and above all is motivated by longing to give you pleasure. Plus there are ways of getting information across without mortally wounding your friend. One of the best is to boost his or her ego in the way you know that he/she likes best.

Annie always moaned her appreciation whenever her man touched her sensual spots, and as he touched the places where she felt best, she emphasised, 'Oh, that's where it's good, that's where it's best. Oh, that's marvellous. Just go on there, that's wonderful right there,' in a skilful combination of natural-sounding delight and masturbation instruction. What she didn't do was say anything negative (such as 'not there. That's the wrong place, can't feel a thing there') and therefore she avoided being discouraging.

It helps if your genitals are slippery. If you are not excited enough to produce your own lubricant, it's a good idea to use spit – yes, plain old ordinary saliva. And if your partner doesn't think of it, then *you* must. There's nothing very difficult about transferring saliva on your hand to your genitals and explaining that it makes everything feel better. If at any stage you experience fears about your partner's reaction, just remind yourself that to your partner you appear as a knowledgeable but loving woman. There's nothing wrong with knowing what to do. And many lovers are relieved by this!

One move you can make is to lovingly guide your partner's fingers over the area that feels best, to give him/her an accurate idea of location, pressure and type of movement. In case this sounds obvious and silly, some lovers, however much they are willing to please, are themselves nervous and lacking in confidence. This doesn't mean they won't be glad to be helped to learn. It does mean you're doing them a favour by teaching them.

Kate eventually showed Ian how she masturbated herself so that he could see what she liked and how she needed it. Elaine, at another workshop, said her boyfriend understood from a similar demonstration just *how long* Elaine needed stimulation for – something he'd not taken in previously.

THE THREATENED LOVER

What happens if your partner feels threatened by your attempts to instruct?

Don't give up but don't let up. Temper your teaching with constant reassurance and words of love and appreciation. If you consistently, again and again, demonstrate with caring, loving affection how marvellous you think he/she is, in time he/she will come round to understanding your needs.

Suppose you struggle on, hammering out love and affection, and months later you still haven't got anywhere with your reassurance? Your partner still apparently feels too threatened to be willing to learn and therefore to try and satisfy you?

This takes you beyond the realm of a sex problem to where, instead, you have reached a personality dispute. If there are enough other aspects of the relationship to make it worth continuing, even without any real sexual input on your partner's side, then naturally it will be worth relying on the vibrator (or fingers) to satisfy your sexual needs. If, however, your partner's inability to learn devastates your hopes of a good relationship, it may be that this partner, sadly, is the wrong one for you. A bad relationship in bed may be a reflection of a bad relationship outside it.

I used to think this a rather high-handed attitude until I heard more and more stories from women in my groups who were so obviously there, not because *they* had problems but because their *men* did. Jan and Jim are good examples of two people who were wrong for each other. Their difficulties and resentments showed up, above all, in the bedroom.

Very often women who come for relationship or sex counselling are non-responsive in bed because they're with the wrong partner. It takes a lot of talking and working out to understand this, and a lot more to actually do something about it. Since marriage problems are outside the range of the pre-orgasmic group, I usually help such women to find a good individual counsellor who can assist them in taking further action in their lives.

MASTURBATION WITH INTERCOURSE

Once your partner has learned how to bring you to climax, either by hand or with a vibrator, you have probably established a highly satisfactory sexual relationship. I personally think this kind of togetherness is every bit as good as a relationship where orgasms come simultaneously as a result of intercourse. But a lot of heterosexual people don't feel the same way. For them, the ultimate is to satisfy each other during intercourse.

The next step, therefore, for those who fall into this camp is to include masturbation with sexual intercourse. Yes, I know it promises broken wrists and all manner of uncomfortable positions, but it can be done very comfortably *once you get used to it*. Listen to what David has to say.

'We like making love with me on top of her in the good old missionary position. We both enjoy this a lot but the only way she can come is by my including my fingers at a certain stage of doing it. I slip my right hand in between our bodies and with my forefinger pointing down along her legs, begin to massage her clitoris while my penis is going in and out of her very slowly. I move my hand much more firmly than my penis and I can keep going like that for a long time without it getting uncomfortable. If my body weight gets a bit much for only one arm to support, I sit back (taking most of my weight on my knees) while my penis is still inside her and this gives even better access to her clitoris.

'Working out what's best for you has got to be a very individual thing. Some positions you simply can't keep up, but with a certain amount of trial and error to begin with, it didn't take us long to find out what was comfortable.'

SELF-STIMULATION DURING INTERCOURSE

Some women prefer to use their own fingers rather than their partner's, and like masturbating themselves to orgasm during intercourse. But what about the women who need that extra added action to really get going?

VIBRATORS DURING INTERCOURSE

The popular image of vibrators tends to be that they are for women only. The belief is that men, faced with an electric-powered plastic penis, rather easily feel rejected. But what gets forgotten here is that a vibrator can be exciting for a man too. The vibrations on sensitive male skin, especially on the scrotum, near the anus, at the base of the penis and on the sides of the penis itself, feel delicious. There are vibrators designed specifically for men. There are also ring-shaped vibrators that slide down the penis to fit around the base and are fantastic to use during intercourse because both partners benefit.

The simplest method of giving you both pleasure, however, is not with some supersonic gadget designed for both sexes. It's a matter of wedging a plain, ordinary vibrator at a tactical point between your genitals (obviously where it is likely to give maximum stimulus to the clitoris) while you are actually making love. David sometimes uses this method with his girlfriend too.

'It never fails,' he says. 'It can sometimes take her ages to come the other way, but this works almost immediately. To make sure the vibrator stays in position between us, I lean forward a bit more so that my weight is always gently pressing it on to her. If it's not in quite the right position, she will move it so that it improves.'

Lesbian women don't need advice about masturbation during intercourse. But the wedging-the-vibrator-between -the-bodies technique is one that would be just as useful for two women making love together.

David's point about the vibrator working where other methods have failed is an important one. American research into vibrator speeds has discovered that the higher the speed of vibration, the easier it is for the woman to climax. Some women, it appears, need a particularly high speed for their orgasm reflex to occur. To those women I would suggest investing in a mains-operated vibrator. They are big and heavy but much more powerful, and therefore a lot more effective.

Vibrator Mini-Survey

Thirty female vibrator users, ages ranging from 22 to 66, were questioned in an attempt to discover what women felt about the vibrator and its relationship to intercourse.

- Slightly more than half said they were as satisfied or more satisfied with a vibrator-induced orgasm as with an orgasm induced by intercourse.

- About a third were less satisfied.

- A small number said 'it depends...' or that the question didn't apply.

- Slightly over half the group used the vibrator for penetration (not necessarily regularly but occasionally).

- Slightly less than half did *not* use the vibrator for penetration.

- Sixteen women had used the vibrator on a partner.

- Only seven women were able to climax by masturbation alone.

- Three of the seven women could *only* climax with a vibrator.

The survey sample was too small to do anything other than provide general indications. What did become clear, though, was that for these women the vibrator was a welcome and diverting aid in relationships. It helped out when the regular partner was away, it solved orgasm problems with women who could have them by no other method, and it provided variety.

PRE-ORGASMIC FOLLOW UP

What is your success rate? What happens to the women who do not learn to climax? These are both questions I'm regularly asked.

FIGURES

Out of eighteen women attending recent groups (none of whom could climax), twelve learned how to, six did not.

In addition, out of a further eight women who attended because they wanted to learn how to have orgasms with their partners – a far more difficult and complicated ambition and not something the groups were designed for – four out of eight managed it occasionally, and the other four began to feel it didn't matter as much as they'd previously thought. Since other parts of their lives had improved as a result of attending, the group could therefore be said to be successful for them, although in a less quantifiable way.

Most major surveys of sexual behaviour since Shere Hite's 1974 report agree that there are between eight and twelve per cent of women who for some reason or other do not experience orgasm. Pre-orgasmic teaching helps some of these women, since their main problem is a lack of knowledge about sex and masturbation.

PHYSICAL SOLUTIONS

But what about those women who just can't seem to experience orgasm at all? Where can they go and what can they do if all this careful homework makes little difference? Fortunately, today this lack of success is seen as a useful diagnostic tool because we now know that there are physical methods of treating such women, depending on what the cause of such complete anorgasmia may be. Not responding to a pre-orgasmic course eliminates ignorance, lack of practice and lack of skill as causes, which helpfully narrows down the problem to some very specific possible causes instead.

There are now specialists in sexual medicine who mainly work in the big teaching hospitals. They work out whether such a woman is affected by:

Inadequate amounts of the hormone testosterone (see Chapter 5) The solution is to be prescribed testosterone in either cream or gel form, which you rub into the skin on a regular basis, or as a patch. Very few doctors will offer a testosterone implant; the slower, more regular method of delivery through the skin, as with cream or gel, is regarded as a better solution.

Depression We now know that libido gets depressed at the same time as general overall depression. This is because the natural body chemicals that come into play during depression lower the natural testosterone levels in the body. The solution is to be prescribed antidepressants and counselling. This is on the grounds that, if you raise the depression, libido normally returns. It must be added that some antidepressants actually make climax difficult, so don't expect too much from this solution until you are off the pills.

Too much inhibition There has been fascinating recent research into brain centres and in particular sexual brain centres, assisted by the newer brain-scan machines that can actually see which parts of your brain 'light up' and which don't. If the bit that ought to be lighting up for sex doesn't do so, or only manages it in a very depleted fashion, then the theory goes that you are suffering from inhibition which actually disables you sexually.

The brain is believed to possess both excitor and inhibitor centres and women are believed to have more than one inhibitor centre, in contrast with men. 'Normal' sexual response is governed in the brain by a careful balance of excitor and inhibitor, but sometimes one or the other malfunctions. If the excitor malfunctions a person may suffer from too many or inappropriate sexual urges (think President Clinton). If the inhibitor malfunctions, this can have the effect of shutting down sexual response. Plus it's now considered that there's a group of women who suffer from a kind of global inhibition that doesn't allow any real sexual feeling to break through. The solution here is a medically prescribed drug called phentolamine that works on the inhibitor centres and frees up sexual sensation.

Drug-related lack of orgasm It is common for women who use opiate-based drugs to experience extreme difficulty in coming to climax. Unfortunately these drugs include methadone, which is commonly used to help heroin addicts go through withdrawal. The solution is easy to write but hard to do. It is to come off opiate drugs completely.

Trauma-induced inhibition The pre-orgasmic groups regularly included women who had been sexually traumatised in some way when younger, that is, they had been abused or raped. Two of these were actually working as sex professionals but had never ever gained any pleasure from the sex act. The solution here was to regard the group as a beginning process and help them find reliable, expert counselling on a long-term basis.

A VALUABLE STARTING POINT

In fact, regarding the group as a beginning process was something we all had to do, teacher and pupils alike. I discovered in the long run that the women would find their way to orgasm *in their own time*; this wasn't something they could do to order, such as within the six-week time limit imposed by the course. Nevertheless, the experience they had in the groups was for all of them a valuable starting point. And the women found it hard to say which they thought was the most important part of the group process. Some declared it to be just being with other women, hearing their stories, feeling their support and learning from them. Some were positive that learning assertion methods changed their entire life, including the ability to climax. Others swore by their trusty vibrators, literally carrying them around in their handbags.

THE WOMEN IN LATER YEARS

So what *did* happen to the women in this book? I followed up the women that my characters are mainly based on, a year later, stayed in touch with a few through further years and managed to gain an overall picture of how life treated them.

HALEY: Haley and her husband didn't manage to survive their open relationship although their sexual difficulties together were largely overcome. Haley emigrated to New Zealand from where she wrote that she found it easier to climax provided she had had a small drink or a spliff. In retrospect, it seems obvious that Haley's problems were to do with inhibition even though from her outgoing behaviour you would never have suspected it.

MAGGIE: Maggie became determined to prove to herself that she could be an effective human being whom people would take seriously. She followed through on her plan to travel out to India, joining her boyfriend again. Excitingly, he turned out to be open to the idea and was pleased to see her. Seven years later they were still together and she sounded like a different woman. She was decisive (the little-girl voice had vanished) and confident. Assertion training had made a world of difference to her.

JAN: Jan's boyfriend, Jim, did leave her shortly after the group ended and Jan had a difficult time for a couple of years, cleaning for other women in order to provide for her little boy. But once he was at school full time she followed her dream by becoming a yoga teacher. She did not find it so easy to make another permanent relationship, and it was over ten years before she moved to a different part of the country and met someone new whom she trusted.

MARY: Mary stayed married to Bruce for the next twenty years and during that time had male lovers with her husband's knowledge. He too had other lovers. But when their children left home, she decided to move in with her long-term lover (with whom she had never had the slightest difficulty in climaxing). Bruce took a while to get over his grief but eventually married the woman *he* had been conducting a long-term relationship with!

MAXIE: Maxie went on to become the personal assistant to a famous lawyer and was integral to helping him produce his various publications. She bought her own very attractive flat in which she lived happily alone. And she met up with a former boyfriend and remade the relationship. This appeared to be much improved from former times as a result of her better mental health. After two years of dating, they married, ran a business together and survived as a married couple for the next twenty years until, sadly, her husband died prematurely.

KATE: Kate was transformed. From being a mouse whom nobody noticed, she grew to be colourful, animated, an original and great fun. Her relationship with Ian lasted for about a year after the group ended. Kate is probably the best person to tell you what proved most important to her from her experience of the group. Here below, are excerpts from Kate's diary.

KATE'S DIARY

THREE WEEKS AFTER THE GROUP ENDED
YES to putting myself first in the discussion about going to Cairo. And NO to going to Cairo and living together without deciding on marriage beforehand. Ian's relatives are in Cairo and he felt it was a big move to take me – tried to seduce me with the idea that this could take the place of a marital commitment. Made love to Ian that morning – he was passive after *he* had come and he lost interest. He was very unstimulated by holding the vibrator to help me come, and left me in the middle of things to phone

someone back – after *he* had come. And he didn't bother to disguise that he was anxious to get things ready for the arrival of our friends. I was unable to come as usual with the vibrator. Was it the atmosphere or was it the batteries? Definitely the former.

THREE MONTHS AFTER THE GROUP ENDED

I've tried to increase the number of different moods I'm in when trying to come to orgasm. Depressed, indifferent, moderately interested in sex. I'm still able to come, less intensely though and it takes longer. I still need vaginal stimulation. This seems to help me. Tried it when Julie was in the other bed. Came in a woman's presence.

I now want to learn to move my body more, when expressing other things. I want to use sexual movement. Now I hope to increase other expressions. A dancer visited our unit the other day – a beautiful mover – fell in love with using the body.

FOUR MONTHS AFTER THE GROUP ENDED

Ian is now beginning to show interest in sharing the vibrator and allowing me to use it during intercourse. I'm near to coming while he's inside me – this is my next and dearest wish.

A WEEK LATER

Ian's word about the timing of his moving in has again and again proved empty. Tonight I told him that I was worried about another bad time if I said 'yes' (giving in to *his* needs) to his coming round. Angrily he told me he would contact me after he'd given his flatmate notice of his leaving. When this has been done I feel I will be able to support him during his seven-days-a-week working. He's been saying one thing to his flatmate and another to me about leaving his flat.

SIX MONTHS AFTER THE GROUP ENDED

Mother died in November. I am closer to my father and Ian has moved in. At first the death of my mother and the practicalities of Ian's move took my energies away. Since a very hectic social life over Christmas and the New Year, we've had more space to ourselves – fear about losing my independence is going.

At first I worried about never having time to myself in bed when I can use the vibrator – now I'm not so worried. Ian stays with his father sometimes – I always use it then. And I think he (we) are beginning to get over the embarrassment of my need for it.

I no longer orgasm in dreams. I no longer dream about women, breasts, etc. Instead I fantasise in my waking life. I'm happy to have erotic images of men now, and sometimes men only – women don't always figure in my fantasies.

A WEEK LATER

Last night I made Ian sit before me and told him to watch me masturbate while I used the vibrator. I couldn't believe he would remain indifferent (as he has done so far) to my coming with it. I told him 'you watch me and I will give you a massage afterwards'. He got quite turned on. Hurrah. After six months – at last my sexiness with the vibrator has affected Ian. Today we made love in the big chair. It was good. I have just signed up for a massage course, as a way of giving me confidence in physical contact that isn't only sexual.

POSTSCRIPT: Eleven months after the group ended

The massage course helped me to make the bridge between companionship/friendship and sex. I am much more confident to touch people now and I express my affection that way. Before the massage course I felt that physical contact would lead inexorably to sex, and of course that's a crazy notion.

As Ian became more mixed up than ever about whether he wanted marriage or not after he moved in, I decided to make a stand and insist on his leaving – he's tried many times to resume the relationship but I feel there's no point in wasting my time over him unless he wants to marry. And I've been able to carry on being assertive with him over this. This is the first time in my life I've ever been able to take this kind of stand with a man. Better late than never! I'm sure it's due to finally feeling confident in myself as a woman. I've changed so much in such a short space of time.

Shortly after this Kate decided to move to a different district, got a promotion as a result, and met a very dishy male colleague. Seven years later, she had two children with him, was busy and happy. Ironically, bearing in mind part of Kate's struggle with Ian, Kate and her new partner have not married.

*

Change can be triggered by many things: a group like mine, a book, a chance remark, a discussion, a traumatic event. But it's never too late. A 66-year-old woman who responded to my vibrator survey made the point that 'too many people think anyone over the age of 35 is kaput'. As she made evident, you are never too old to begin enjoying sex, masturbation and vibrators. She tried her first vibrator out at the age of 59 and loved it.

INDEX